The Official Biography

Tom Savini

Additional Material by Michael Aloisi

Interior Design by: Darin Peters and Alicia C. Mattern

Cover Design by: Alicia C. Mattern

Cover Photo Credit: Ama Lea

Published by Dark Ink, 2019, in Southwick, MA.

www.DarkInkBooks.com

Dark Ink and its logo are trademarked by AM Ink Publishing.

I am in my seventies now and since I intend to live to be around a hundred and ten; I am more than halfway through, so it's time I jot down my life so far. Many miracles landed on me and changed me, guided me, and created me. I was almost killed at least five times that I can remember, and this makes me think I am supposed to be here for a bit longer. I fully believe, like all of you, that before it is my time to go, they will discover eternity and I won't have to leave.

– Tom Savini –

Table of Contents

In spite of being aware of the fact that,
it's not interesting just because it happened to you,
here's what happened to me…

– Tom Savini –

I Was Born When I Was Very Young

I was born when I was very young. I know this sounds like a joke, BUT... if being born is when your awareness takes over your body, when you become conscious, and in my case, when you suddenly wake up into your surroundings... then it happened to me when I was almost a year old. I kind of popped into existence. My very first memory.

I was walking in the kitchen of my house, and I was surrounded by many boxes filled with my parent's goodies because they were just moving in. I was very aware, and very intelligent, and I felt like I knew so much about everything, and I also felt like I was just somewhere else, someplace different just moments before, like waking up from a dream and forgetting what the dream was.

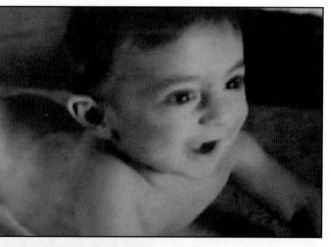

So what was this little body, this mindless, soulless little physical specimen walking around in this kitchen, before I invaded it? It doesn't matter, because all this awareness I was experiencing, all this intelligence, this all-knowing insight into what I was seeing surrounding me disappeared the moment my father started chasing me around the house, then yelling at me from atop the basement stairs, after I fled down there... because I had crapped in my pants.

Suddenly I was no longer this bright little being entering the world, but this little child with a mess in his pants, his father's voice reducing him into the toddler he is supposed to be now. This is why I believe in reincarnation and why I say I truly was born when I was very young.

Playing on my street in winter

Our neighborhood pool

First Communion, Age 7

I am in my early seventies now and since I intend to live to be around a hundred and ten, I am a little more than halfway through life so it's time I jot down what has happened so far. Many miracles landed on me and changed me, guided me, and created me. I almost died or was killed at least five times that I can remember, and this makes me think I am supposed to be here for a bit longer. I fully believe, like all of you, that before it is my time to go, before it is my time to die, they will discover eternity and I won't have to leave.

I won't pull any punches, and I'll never lie to you, so I hope you can take it. There will be topics that describe certain parts of my life that include:

The Day I Was Kidnapped

The Traveling Horror Show

How To Deal with Bullies

The Night We Saw a Flying Saucer

How Lon Chaney Changed My Life Forever

What It's Like Being The Godfather of Gore, The King of Splatter

My Internet Date Nightmare

My Encounter with The Paranormal

On Working with Quentin Tarantino

Staring at Salma Hayak's Ass for Three Days

On Having The Number One Makeup School in The World

How I Met and Worked with George Romero

Becoming Sex Machine in From *Dusk Till Dawn*

How My Movie Career Began

There is Also...

How I Almost Died or Was Killed Five Times

I Smoked A Joint with Timothy Leary

Google Says I Am a Dick

...and Many, Many More

I am the baby of the family with four older brothers and an older sister, she being the youngest of that clan with thirteen years between us. I slept in the attic at my house, and I guess it was sort of an initiation. All my brothers, and probably my older sister, had to sleep up there.

No heat at all from the house below came up to visit the attic. There was this door to a storage room held upright against the frame by a nail that was bent and pulled over one edge of the door. The wind would come into the storage area through a vent and that door would rattle, so of course there were hideous monsters behind the door trying to get me. It was so cold up there that I would have to take the mattress

Richard and Diane Savini, me center

Henry

Joe

Sullivan

12

Henry

off the other bed and pull it up over me to stay warm, thereby preventing any monsters from getting me.

I also had my rocket-shaped crystal radio. It had an alligator clip at the end of a wire that came out of it that I could clip to a metal floor grate and get the local stations through the earplug. I would fall asleep every night under the warm mattress listening to late night DJ's and pop music.

I had five fathers: my real father and my four older brothers, and two mothers: my real one and my older sister. My father was 50 when I was born and my mother was 42. I was a "change-of-life baby." My poor sister Rose had to have me by her side almost always. Being by her side on Sundays meant watching her copy the Sunday funnies from the Sunday paper with her little colored pencils. Side by side, when she was done, you couldn't tell the difference between the comic characters in the paper and the copies she drew of them. To me, that was impossible. A miracle. How the hell could she do that? It was my first glimpse into the world of talented artists.

Rose

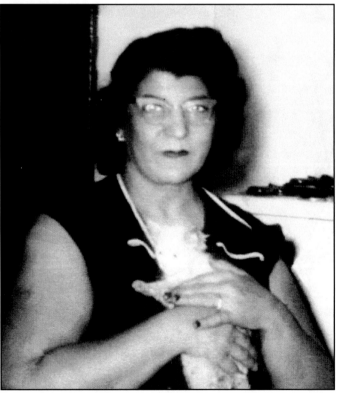
Mum

My second glimpse was of my older brother Henry, who was 92 when he passed away. He was studying to be a mortician and I would see him sculpting clay into a fabulous Egyptian head or something, practicing his restorative skills. I would sit there for hours watching him, and taking my own little blobs of clay and trying to make something. I believed when I made a little woman, I could lift the clay off her belly and there would be a little clay baby.

I spent my early childhood copying my brothers and sister and trying to be like them. Henry was the smart guy. He smoked a pipe, sculpted, read books, tattooed people, and listened to classical music. Sullivan was into physical fitness. He was the strong, muscular type and looked the most like my mother. Joe had this amazing sense of humor and was always making me laugh. Tony, who died when I was 13, was a male nurse with special clients like a County Commissioner. He was the quiet type and was into tape recorders and music. Rose was my sister/babysitter who hung out with her girlfriends next door, took me to movies, and copied the funny papers. I am a composite of them all.

But my father was the adhesive. He could do anything. I grew up watching this man be very good at many things and thought it was just normal to do many things well. I thought everyone was supposed to do many things well.

He was a carpenter, a bricklayer, an electrician, a plumber, and even a shoemaker. He had all the tools including the shoe block to make repairs on our shoes. He even made toys for us at Christmas like an articulating, wooden dancing puppet. In his later years, his hands shook and he was frustrated with not being able to make stuff. I followed him around without him knowing it and shot video. I have hours and hours of him peacefully smoking his pipe, planting his garden, or planing wood to make cabinets, or through the kitchen window I'd tape him making homemade ravioli. I would shoot through kitchen windows or out my bedroom window. He never knew, and whenever I want him now... I just have to put the video in the player. My mother was a three hundred pound foul-mouthed... angel... saint.

Young Mum

Rose

The Day I Was Kidnapped

kay I will spit this out short and sweet. When I was around seven I was kidnapped. I was walking up to this place called Isaly's to get an ice cream cone. This guy blocked my path in his car and said "Where are you going?" I said I was going to get some ice cream. He said, "Want a ride?" I know... classic case. I got in his car and we traveled into some wooded desolated area. I wondered where we were going and he said he knew a better place to get ice cream. Well... he did things to me and made me do things to him. No penetration, and I learned some new words... and I cried because I knew he was going to kill me like all kidnapped children. I wasn't stupid. I remember peeing in his mouth... what the hell did I know about cumming? Later he drove me home, but first bought me a pint of ice cream. He dropped me off where he picked me up, and on the way home I threw the ice cream as far as I could throw. I remember it landing, smashing and sliding, leaving a trail behind it as it traveled into the street. It was dark, and my parents were very worried, and I told them just that some guy bought me ice cream. I could see they knew what that meant, and my mother started rattling off names like "Andy...that son of a bitch... wait 'til I see him at the bowling alley." They never mentioned it again. I never saw the man again, but I think of him often. Since that day I have never had any bad feelings toward gay men or women and have lots of gay friends. I don't try to say "Oh, poor me, I was an abused child," or blame any shit on that traumatic sexual abuse I suffered as a child. It happened. I realized then that these things happen. I came out of it okay. I don't hate gays... just perverts. The really good thing that came out of that experience is the way I am with women. I don't force myself on anyone. I really don't want to intrude. I, almost like a mythical vampire, need to be invited across the threshold. I need to be invited across a woman's threshold. I don't make the first move. I need to be invited. Don't get me wrong, I look for the invitation, and if it's there, I proceed confidently, and I don't like to force myself as I remember what it was like to have someone force himself on me, the rough beard stubble on my face and such, and I never ever want anyone to feel that from me.

GRANDE ILLUSIONS

The Art and Technique of Special Make-Up Effects
Original Books I & II

From The Films of

TOM SAVINI

Forewords by: Stephen King, George Romero and Dick Smith

I went to elementary school with guys named Rocco Massochetti, Tony Persichetti, Nino Orsini, Richard Porco, Beatrice Roberto, and Ed Rainaldi. You getting all the vowels here? Just recently they renamed my neighborhood Little Italy, something I always wanted them to do.

You could walk through my neighborhood of Bloomfield and on every corner there were these little Italian guys gyrating and using their hands, speaking Italian. When my father and I walked up the street, occasionally he would be engaged by them, and all I would see was him emphatically throwing his hands into the air, conducting a conversation back and forth with them. I understood a lot of this because when I was a child, I spoke Italian. In fact, I had to learn English. Today I don't remember much of it, though when I go to Rome, it just comes out. If I am lost, I walk up to a policeman and suddenly to my surprise, blurt out in perfect Italian a request for directions. It's in here in my head somewhere, and I hope to release it with The Diplomatic Course in Italian that I bought a few years ago, or the recently purchased Rosetta Stone.

Okay, so I was loafing on the corner in what is now Little Italy, watching cars and girls go by, talking about unimportant crap with whoever else had nothing better to do, going to the movies on Saturdays and watching TV and being scared by monsters, and being bullied by the bullies, and on one of those Saturdays... I saw *Man of a Thousand Faces*.

I have to make this more important. *MAN OF A THOUSAND FACES*. Somehow even this isn't important enough to describe what happened to me. It would have been the same if a hypnotist put me in trance that lasted a lifetime. Wherever I went, I was deeply and constantly thinking about that movie, walking around as if in a trance, thinking about that movie.

I had loved monsters even when they scared the shit out of me. I believed they were real. That's what made them scary... they were real. BUT with this movie, I suddenly realized that of course, someone was creating them. The

The True Story of the Life and Loves of LON CHANEY!

Universal International presents

JAMES CAGNEY
DOROTHY MALONE
JANE GREER

"MAN OF A THOUSAND FACES"

CinemaScope

movie, if you don't know, was about the life of Lon Chaney. I named my first and only son Lon. Lon Chaney was a silent movie actor, stuntman, and most of all, superb makeup

Me as Ben Franklin in *1776*

artist, who created such roles as Quasimo-do, the Hunchback of Notre Dame; Erik, the Phantom of the Opera, and many, many more. James Cagney played Lon Chaney and this was the first time the thought that monsters are created by people entered my head. Before that, they were real. Frankenstein was some scary guy sewn together from body parts of people, and when he came to life, he was the scariest thing my eyes had ever seen. But this movie, this *Man of a Thousand Faces*, showed me they don't exist on their own; they are not real. They are makeup and special effects and actors portraying them and so... little did I realize that it was the end of that particular magic of seeing through innocent eyes and believing something to be real. The result? I then wanted to make them. I wanted to make monsters. I wanted to know how to use makeup and create monsters and scary faces. I wanted to make them. I wanted to be different people, perhaps by putting on makeup.

My Universal Monster Sculptures

This was the beginning of the end of the magic that I had experienced before that, the magic that I would love to experience again somehow. I believed they were real, really existed on the screen, in the dark alleys of Bloomfield, and behind that flimsy door in my attic. This is the irony that people who want to be involved in the movies experience; the magic that you see and feel that makes you want to be involved in movies is destroyed and gone forever once you are involved. Not completely, mind you, but that purest form of it, when you really believe what you are seeing is real, is somehow gone. I wish I could see a movie again through a child's eyes, an unaffected child's eyes, so I could see and feel and believe again in that purest sense.

creation that someone wants you to enjoy. However, the magic does come back. If a movie is really good, really engaging, the magic does come back sometimes. Like some of Spielberg's movies, really good filmmaking makes you think and feel and complete the thoughts and emotions or actions of the characters in your own mind. It comes back if I see the movie about eight times, or more easily if I just smoke a joint and see it stoned. Focused.

So, I was a teenager wanting to learn makeup. Where? There were no schools back then that I knew of. There was this stage makeup book at the library by Richard Corson that became my bible. It was stage

I used to say I wish I could see a movie through my daughter Lia's eyes, but she is just as "tainted" as I am, almost. She made me take her to see Coppola's *Dracula* a number of times because she liked it so much. I am sure there were people in the audience saying to themselves, "What is that grown man doing here with that little child?" Lia was around nine or so, but if you had sat next to her and heard the conversation you would have heard her say things like "Dad, is that a blue screen effect or real? Is that foam latex or gelatin? Is that real hair or yak hair?" "Shut up!" I would whisper. It's hard enough for me to see a movie and NOT think about all that stuff.

You see what I mean? Where the thought goes? How to create it, instead of enjoying that it is a

 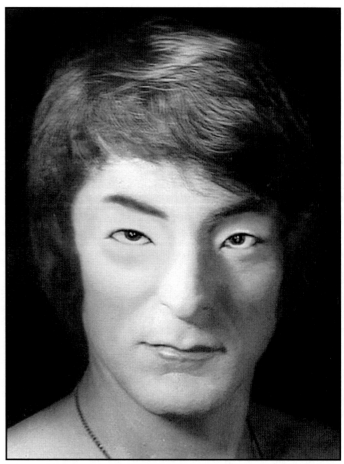

makeup: overdone. You had to overdo it because of the distance of the audience from the actors and the brightness of the lights. But it did talk about latex, and spirit gum, and crepe hair, and mortician's wax, and greasepaint, and a few other staples of the trade. It told me enough so I would know what to buy if I could ever find a store. My brother Tony told me about a store that sold theatrical makeup downtown. Back then it could have been on the moon. Downtown? That was the big city, the big place with all the buildings and big streets and noisy traffic, a place that a little kid like me could only go when his father would take him on a streetcar and pay money and travel there... like going to another country. That would be too big of an adventure for a little kid like me: a little poor kid who only got into a car when an older brother or relative came by to take us somewhere.

And, you had to have money to buy that stuff. So that was it: I had to have money. We could take soda pop bottles back to the store then and turn them in for the deposit of two cents each, five cents if it was one of those big soda bottles. But it would take too long to look for and collect them and you really didn't make a lot of money that way. So, I put together a shoe-shine kit with the little money I could get from the bottles and started around the neighborhood shining shoes, and wow, I was really making a lot of money. I forget now what I was charging back then but it started to pile up. It was enough so that I could take a streetcar downtown — yep, all by myself — and search for Essers Costumes where they sold makeup.

I walked in, and there, for the first time, the smell of the greasepaint entered my nostrils and my life. I still feel a thrill when I open one of my makeup kits and smell the makeup. I bought crepe hair, my color, some spirit gum, some latex and some collodion. Collodion is what is used in movies to create scars. You brush it on, it attaches itself to your skin, dries, and starts to contract, leaving a deep, temporary crease in your skin. Think Tom Berenger in *Platoon* or Donald Pleasance as the villain in *You Only Live Twice*.

I began experimenting on myself. A big mistake.

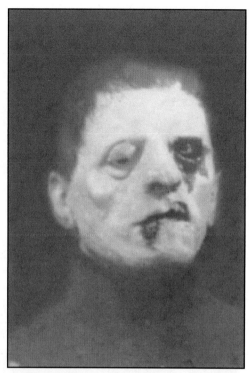

I would go to school with half my eyebrows missing or a blob of nose putty stuck in my hair for a week. So, I began experimenting on my little playmates. I would cut their wrists open using mortician's wax and fake blood or make them look like half of their hair was burned off or their throats were cut. They would go home, and of course, their parents, not thinking about makeup when their children walked into the house maimed by me, would scream "who the hell did that to you"...the answer was "Savini" and for a while they weren't allowed to play with me.

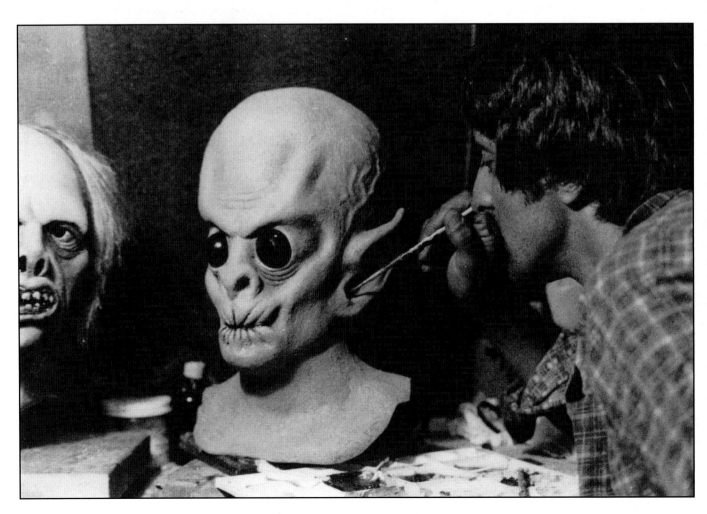

Speaking of magic, when I was around 13 or 14 there was an ad in the paper: "Live from Hollywood: Frankenstein, the Wolfman, and Dracula, and a magic show and a horror movie double feature"...all at the Arsensal theater. WHAT!!!???? Frankenstein, the Wolfman, AND Dracula? You gotta be kidding! Of course, I was there before the theater opened and the first thing was a magic act. It was Dr. Silkini. Dr. Silkini was like the Dread Pirate Roberts from *The Princess Bride*. The original guy was no longer and a succession of younger magicians would take turns becoming him. He was a famous magician in his time. He made doves appear and did things with flowers and had a few mechanical things to make up his magic act.

Then, at some point, he would cue someone in the theater and the lights would go down slightly. A guy in a Frankenstein mask would come out from one side, and from the other side, a guy in a Wolfman mask would come out...and then Dracula, who was a kid they picked out of the audience, would come out and just stand there, full of stage fright. Just stand there! Frank and the Wolfman would meet center stage and it looked like they were going to fight, but at the last moment, they looked into the audience and then came down the steps toward us...and the lights would go out. Everyone screamed and swore the monsters were lurking among them. After a minute or two of this, the double feature horror movies would start: *Night Of The Blood Beast* or something. Well, jolly good, that was fun, but they picked a kid out of the audience to play Dracula? I swore I was coming back tomorrow and they were going to pick me.

I already had my own cape and fangs and makeup kit, and they picked this dolt who just stood there? I hoped to change that. I was back the next day and I must have waved my hand or screamed just right because they did pick me. I explained I had my own fangs and cape and was already dabbling in makeup but they rushed me to a drug store and bought this stuff called Sudden Beauty and the magician, whose name was Gabriel, had a lovely female assistant named Dinah, and she smeared it all over my face and when it dried it cracked and I looked like a broken porcelain doll and it was great. I had never heard of this stuff. Then they did this beautiful vampire makeup on me with black lips and dark eyes and sunken cheekbones and I felt like I had just been made up by a professional Hollywood make-up artist. I used my own fangs. I also learned that Frankenstein was named Chuck, and the Wolfman was Donald.

It was showtime. Dr. Silkini did his act and it was time for the monsters. This was the moment I learned about misdirection. I was hiding down front, right behind dark curtains at the one of the exits. I was peering through the curtains and saw the audience was looking far to the right at Frankenstein; then the Wolfman came out, and when I saw that the audience was looking at the Wolfman, I sneaked out and up to the

front row of kids with my cape pulled over hiding me, and when it was my cue, I leaped into the air with my cape outstretched and totally took them by surprise as if I just appeared there. They screamed and you could see all of them fly backwards in their seats. I scared the fuck out of them and for a moment, Gabriel, Chuck, Donald, and Dinah SAW what I had done with my entrance.

They no longer picked a kid out of the audience for the rest of their tour of local movie theaters: they took me with them. I became part of the troupe. It was so much fun hanging out with them at their hotel and at restaurants, and I learned my first lessons in magic from Gabriel. They traveled in a big black hearse, and I remember, one day I was riding around with them and there was nothing in the hearse but a thin black table. It couldn't have been any thicker than an inch and a half. I kept hearing "Cooooo....Coooo..." and I asked, "What is that? Gabe said, "Oh that's just the doves inside the table." The doves were kept inside that way so that when they appeared in the act, they would flutter and flap their wings. It made for a better entrance. On one occasion hanging out with Chuck, he told me the acne on his face was because he hadn't had sex for a while being on this tour. I missed the troupe when they had to leave town. They paid me in silver dollars and chocolate milk shakes.

What they left behind was what I learned from them. I learned a lot but the most important thing was the misdirection I used for my entrance, waiting for the audience to look elsewhere before I scared the shit out of them. That was an important discovery I would use over and over again in my career. Also, I learned the value of magic, which is full of misdirection and mechanical devices, the same as makeup effects. We do the same thing as magicians. We misdirect you and we have lots of mechanical devices to make you think what you are seeing is really happening. Misdirection is important when you want to fool or scare people. That is why I named my two books on makeup effects *Grande Illusions*. I think of this stuff as magic tricks.

Years later, a great many years, I was trying to become a member of The Magic Castle in Hollywood. It's a private club only for magicians since around 1926, located in a beautiful mansion on Franklin Avenue in Los Angeles behind the famous Grauman's Chinese Theater. You have to be a magician to be a member. As a kid, I would read in Famous Monsters Magazine how Boris Karloff had just appeared there to record an album of scary stories or some other incredible "happening" there in the land I would never get to know as Los Angeles/Hollywood. But it was Dr. Silkini, now another guy, who sponsored me into The Magic Castle. We were communicating at the time about a vampire script they were trying to get produced. I was going to do the effects. It also didn't hurt that I had written two books titled *Grande Illusions*. Thanks to him, to this day I am a card-carrying member of The Magic Castle.

The Night We Saw A Flying Saucer

I was a kid in the fifties and that was the heyday of science fiction movies like *The Thing from Another World, War of the Worlds, Invasion of the Saucermen, Earth vs. the Flying Saucers, This Island Earth, Forbidden Planet.* Visitors from another planet was a recurring theme, and back then, before I realized somebody has to create this stuff, IT WAS REAL. I BELIEVED EVERYTHING I SAW ON THE MOVIE SCREEN WAS REAL. When you're nine or ten years old, it is as much a part of your little life as Santa Claus or the Tooth Fairy. They exist until some smart-ass older kid convinces you they don't.

One night in my neighborhood, just a few blocks from my house at Friendship Park, (Friendship Park was a quiet zone two or three blocks long, the entire length of The Immaculate Conception elementary school housing for the priests and nuns, plus the huge buildings that made up the Western Pennsylvania Hospital and its housing for nurses) while teens played football and necked on the park benches.... WE ALL SAW A FLYING SAUCER. It scared the living shit out of us. We froze... it was really happening... a thousand thoughts attacking us at once like: we have to alert the world, call the army, run and hide, warn our parents.... meet the aliens. We couldn't speak; we were in shock. We were paralyzed with fear. When we finally could move and speak, we screamed at people who weren't looking

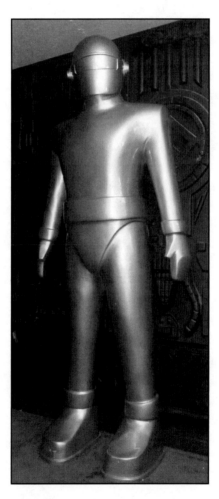

to look up.... LOOK...UP THERE... LOOK! Above the hospital, brightly lit and spinning, it was traveling in a straight line and flying low. The park went crazy. People were running into each other and back and forth across the grassy center section not knowing what the hell to do, thinking about the horrible things that happen to hapless civilians in the movies when the aliens land. We thought it was going to land right there in Friendship Park just like the flying saucer in *The Day the Earth Stood Still.*

To me it was thrilling and otherworldly, and I felt like I was a part of something really big, like in the movies. No longer was I unconnected, sitting in a movie theater watching something dramatic... but connected and actually living the drama. Lots of teenagers and kiddies and adults running and screaming in a park while a bright and colorful spinning flying saucer hovered over them, about to destroy us or land and its occupants demand that we take them to our leaders. I was standing my ground, staring, soaking it up, making the most of every second before the laser blast would eventually hit and disintegrate us. Even my imagination-filled childish eyes could see after a moment or two that this dream that was finally happening to me and people I know... was actually an airplane dragging a long sign behind it.

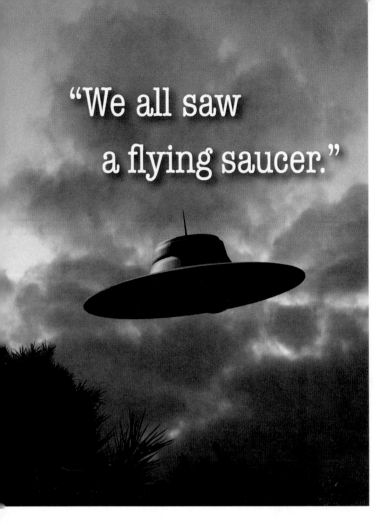

"We all saw a flying saucer."

Iron is not on the tv while I work out: it makes me feel like I am working out with Arnold and his friends. And here he was, on the phone. It was amazing. We spoke for like fifteen minutes, and I was amazed that he knew so much of my career and was a fan, which is not too out of the ordinary as I am constantly surprised when I meet celebrities and they tell me they are fans of mine. So here I was, happily having this great conversation with Arnold, who was telling me I have to do more effects in my career and such stuff, and for a good hour after we hung up, I was glowing and bragging about speaking with Arnold and bouncing around with a big smile on my face and thanking Rob for setting it up. Eventually Rob, who was afraid I would be pissed off at him that it wasn't real, came to me and told me how sorry he was, that this was a friend impersonating Arnold, and please don't be mad at him. I said I was not mad…because for those fifteen minutes, I believed it. The feeling was real. I really thought I was talking to Arnold. To me it was real: just like that flying saucer. Years later, at the Arnold Classic, I met Arnold and he knew who I was!

You couldn't see the plane because a huge light was focused and shining from behind the plane on the sign. The wind made the sign wave in the darkness, creating the optical illusion of it spinning. So all we saw was this brightly lit, spinning…THING… flying across the black star-filled sky in the days when the local movie theater played nothing but science fiction classics. But, for that moment, when we looked and believed, it was splendid; it was thrilling. I really had the feeling in me that there was a flying saucer flying above me and my friends. I can still feel it. That was the important thing…that feeling…false or not…for those moments I felt it and believed it. It was real for those few moments.

It reminds me now of my friend Rob Lucas, who knows this guy who can do a perfect Arnold Schwarzenegger impression. Not a stereotypical one but a full-on conversational Arnold. He's been on the Tonight Show and can also do and look like Robert De Niro. Anyway, we were at a convention and Rob came up to me excited and smiling and told me he had Arnold on the phone and wanted to talk to me. I was stupefied. Arnold is my hero. Not a day goes by in my home gym when *Pumping*

Always Home

t's hard to explain, but even as a kid of maybe ten years old, I remember sitting on the floor in my dad's bedroom and the house talked to me. Not really of course, but I did feel a bonding taking place. Looking around at the walls and the decor that my dad had established with the dark wooden closets he built...I thought to myself that I would be here a long time. And I have. When I die, my ghost will probably hang around here for a while and not leave. It's the same with the neighborhood. I have so many friends who have moved away and set up house in other places and the one thing I can say about myself that they don't have is that I have never lost my sense of home. I am still in the house I was born and raised in and still in the ever-changing neighborhood, but I know these alleys and all the nooks and crannies. There are still the Italians on the corner talking with their hands. They are much older and their children are now adults that I sometimes recognize, and some of the restaurants are still here, and I feel I get strength in the knowledge that I didn't have to move away to make my dreams come true. All of the work, all of my accomplishments, all of my fame: I obtained it while still living in my hometown, in my home.

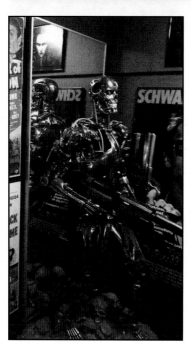

The Magic Of Movies

And oh yes....the MOVIES! The motivation for everything I do. THE MOVIES. What a silly word. If there's a lot of salt, it is saltY, or something is chalkY, or milkY, or soapY or snowY or...if it moves... it is a MOVIE. We add the Y/eee sound to make it a new word. FILM...CINEMA...MOTION PICTURES... nope... a movie. How sophisticated of us. I prefer to call them what Louie B. Mayer and other studio heads called them: "Pictures." They made "Pictures."

You know what? THESE ARE THE GOOD OLD DAYS. When you look back and say those were the good old days, you are also thinking, *I wish I was back there*, or *When I was there, I wish I had enjoyed it more*. Well, you are here now, and soon you won't be, so to avoid ever thinking that way again...THESE ARE THE GOOD OLD DAYS...right now...get it?

But, back in the good old days, my favorite part of this fantasy I call my life was the Fifties. I don't live in the past but I play my memories in my mind like they are favorite songs or something. I was a little kid in the Fifties, and I lived for Saturday. I'd wake up at seven in the morning, rush downstairs, grab a box full of cereal, and sit down in front of our big black and white television and watch *Tom Terrific, Sky King, Mighty Mouse, Winky Dink, Howdy Doody, Captain Midnight, Buster Brown Theater*, and *Jungle Jim*, and all this before noon; then a Tarzan movie, and Walt Disney's *Davy Crockett*.

But on some very special Saturdays, it was the neighborhood Plaza Theater, where you went in around nine in the morning and joined a theater full of screaming kids your age and saw seventeen cartoons, and I'm talking about *Merrie Melodies* and *Looney Tunes*, (I can still hum the difference in their similar theme songs), and *Popeye* and Warner Brothers and Max Fleischer cartoons: Bugs Bunny, Daffy Duck, Porky Pig, and Foghorn Leghorn. And after all that screaming and applauding every time a new cartoon started, we would see a serial like *Captain Marvel*, or *Commando Cody*, or *The Ape and The Robot*. Then, after the preview of coming attractions, we would see two, yes two, FEATURE LENGTH FILMS, like the *House of Wax* or *Abbott and Costello Meet Frankenstein*, and all of this for a quarter. Twenty-five cents!

We would come out of the theater around five in the afternoon and the daylight would hurt our eyes walking home because we were sitting in the

31

dark all day, and when we got home, the television seemed like some insignificant nightlight. In the winter, it would be dark out when we left the theater, and the flying saucers and aliens and monsters and *The Teenage Frankenstein* was surely in every dark corner on the way home. I say "we" because it was usually me and my older sister, who would confirm at every step of the walk home that monsters were going to get me.

Those were my early childhood weekends. The weekdays were school and nuns slapping the piss out of us and bullies and comic books, like Superman and Batman and Little Lulu, and hot dogs, and summer days at the local swimming pool. I used to pretend I lived in a mansion and would leave my house and walk the downhill block to the pool, pretending I was walking down my lane or driveway to MY pool. Once there, I pretended to wonder why all these people were in my pool. Ah...guests.

Halloween was the most important day of the year... still is. I keep a 1969 newspaper in my collection. In the entertainment section is the movie listings for over fifty drive-in theaters around Pittsburgh. Fifty!!! Now that was magic. There were probably more back in my precious Fifties. My parents never had a car, but sometimes one of my four older brothers would take a girlfriend or wife and haul us kids in the backseat. "Where are we going?" we'd say. "To the Drive-In," they'd say. Oooooo... silent glee in the backseat. Are you kidding?! We park the car and eat popcorn and outside on that big screen they'd show us a motion picture....a MOVIE!!!!!

See it's hard to do: calling them "Pictures." But that is today. Back then, they were "Movies" and they were magic. A movie theater was magic. I didn't see them as buildings of wood and concrete. Here was a place off the street you walked into and it wasn't where you took your clothes to get them dry cleaned, it wasn't the supermarket, and it wasn't the hardware store. Those places had their purposes but what was the purpose of this movie theater thing? Magic. Where you were transported to other times and dimensions and met vampires and werewolves and outer space aliens and horrible scary monsters and become the hero and saved the world and it was all very real. Like a church where you adored what was up there where the altar should

be: it was magic. MAGIC. A place, unlike a book or the radio where you create the sets and characters in your mind, it was all up there for you.

I still today get very upset when a movie theater closes down. My neighborhood theater The Plaza is where most of my movie magic happened my whole childhood. It opened in 1917, and only a few years ago closed down for good to become...Starbucks. You know I hate Starbucks. There was another theater a healthy walk away called The Arsenal. I say healthy because after going up a short hill, you plunged around five or six long blocks downhill to another neighborhood called Lawrenceville. When the movie was over you had to walk up those blocks to get home. I was usually the one kid in my neighborhood, at age 12, that led another group of kids, all around the age of 9 or 10, on the long trek to The Arsenal. When it closed down, to me it was a house of magic that didn't exist anymore. I don't understand. How could people let such a thing go away? Don't you want to keep that magic in your lives?

I still think of movie theaters as houses of magic where you worship that magic, but it's very hard today to go to movie theaters. I really hardly ever go to a movie theater now, and not because I have created my own little home theater with my big ten-foot screen and high def 3D projector. No, it's because of all the anxiety I have to go through in a movie theater wondering how many people I am going to have to tell to shut the fuck up or turn off that cell phone. But I try to be polite: "No offense, but you have to be quiet now," or "No offense, but you have to turn that off in here." If I am lucky, they remember vaguely seeing the not-so-effective little notice that came up before the movie about not talking or texting. There's gotta be a convention of theater owners somewhere to whom you can make a big deal about theaters doing more to make people shut the fuck up and not use their phones. This is a house of magic, damn it! That's why I love the Alamo Drafthouse Cinema franchise. They warn you and threaten you fifty times before the movie and if you try to use your cell phone or talk, you will just about be arrested, or at least thrown out. Good on them.

Trying To Lose My Virginity

After months of trying to fuck Carol H........, it finally happened with another girl, at the ripe old age of thirteen. "In school tomorrow... if anyone asks you....say you got laid last night," Tony said. Tony was my agent, my procurer, my pimp for a night. A thirteen year old Italian grade school classmate who was the force, the instigator...HE MADE IT HAPPEN; to me, the not so man of the world, hip teenager that the rest of my friends seemed to be. But back to Carol.

Carol H......... was a neighborhood girl who through my cousin V.........., allowed us to take her under a bridge into some caves, get naked, and have sex. We were twelve or thirteen years old. We would take turns. When it was my turn I was very turned on and ready and hard but I couldn't find an opening on her. She would guide me and hold me in a place, but I never felt I was entering her. From the photos I saw in Playboy or something I assumed you entered a woman face to face and through the very top of the vagina. I didn't know that you entered more down-hill than that, directly between the legs and under the pubic hump. So I tried and tried to enter from above, and I guess she just put up with it, thinking me some feckless ignorant idiot, because when it was my cousin's turn, they didn't sound like they were having a clumsy time of it.

Then one night Tony P................. and I were walking in Friendship Park, the park with the flying saucer if you remember, and he saw some girl we knew to belong to the neighborhood named Olga. He said she was promiscuous, or in his terms, "laying guys." He said to wait, and he walked up to her and said a few things, his hands waving in the air. Not odd because we were little Italian kids who didn't speak unless our hands looked like we conducting a symphony, emulating our fathers. Soon he came back to me and said, "Let's go." With Olga in the lead, we searched back alleys near our grade school, The Immaculate Conception. I swear to God that was the name of my elementary school and I repeat: The Immaculate Conception. "Hey, where do you go to school?" friends would ask. The simple and understood reply was "Mac."

She indicated a dark backyard right there in the alley. I thought cars or people might see us when they passed by. Tony said, "No fucking way," and we proceeded.

What a turn on. I could see her taking off her skirt and lying down behind some shrubs. Tony went behind with her and I could hear them so by the time it was my turn I was really, really ready. I went back there as Tony went to keep watch and saw her lying there half naked. In those days a large amount of pubic hair was normal, and it tickled. Then she guided me and for the first time in my life I felt what it was like to be INSIDE a woman, and it was so warm and so tickling beyond endurance and exciting. When I reached orgasm I pulled out, having the presence of mind not to get her pregnant. I was no longer a virgin. Back then, that was the same as a scarlet letter that you wore in shame. I was now a man and strutted it proudly the next day at school and didn't miss an opportunity to tell all, "last night I got laid."

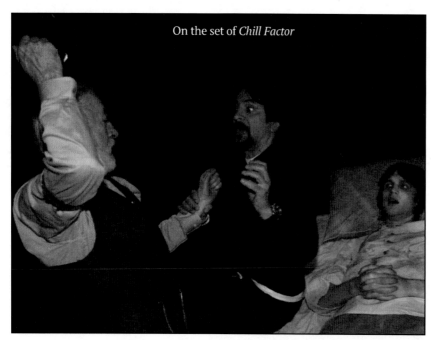
On the set of *Chill Factor*

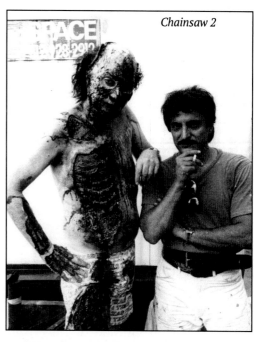
Chainsaw 2

Chop-Top (Bill Moseley) cuts Gino

Chainsaw 2

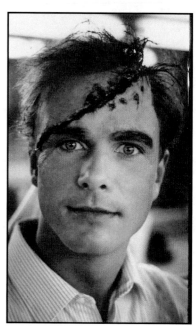

How I Met and Worked with George Romero

I went to an all-boys high school. Coats and ties every day. There were 1500 of us taught by Christian Brothers. Ex-cops, ex-marines, and some of the toughest guys you ever could meet. There were also some of the gentlest men you could meet. Comedians, actors, and what made for a really varied and interesting experience. They wore robes like priests but their collar was two white short slabs that protruded from under their chins.

This was *the* high school. None of my brothers went there. They went to trade schools if at all, but my dad was insistent that his youngest son, me, go there. I was surrounded by mostly rich kids from well-to-do families, and it was very expensive, but my dad made it happen.

Brother Leonard was the biggest and toughest. If he caught you talking in class, he would approach you as he wrapped a handkerchief around his fist. "Stand up," he would grunt, and once you did he asked if you wanted "6 inches or 12?" It didn't matter what you said but you probably said "6." Then he would say, "Alright... clench your teeth so I don't break your jaw." Now you would be scared shitless but you certainly clenched your teeth. Pow... he punched you in the face. Not really hard, but enough to scare the hell out of you, jar you, and make sure you didn't talk out of turn again.

Brother Patrick would teach us Latin and wander around the classroom with a piece of chalk in his hand. Occasionally, he'd pick up someone's book, someone who was probably not paying attention, and with the chalk he would write on the book whatever he was trying to demonstrate. We all thought that was hilarious.

Brother Benedict would play a recording of *Macbeth* and pull his black robe over his head and act out the witches' scene for us. We called him Black Benny.

The other Brother Benedict, who had white hair, was White Benny and he taught us typing. Three monumental things happened to change my life while I was at Central Catholic: I met George Romero, I learned to type, and John F. Kennedy was assassinated.

I was very active in high school: on the track team, in the band, on the wrestling team, and most of all, in the theater. We had a great professional theater there and only did musicals like *Guys and Dolls, Once upon a Mattress, Bye Bye Birdie*, which I

The mob in Rio watches the Latin footwork of Tom Savini and Mary Lou Murphy.

The Beast and his Better: Harry the Horse (Gene

choreographed just before I graduated, and *Where's Charley*. I was usually the lead dancer, and in a few of them, had a featured dancing part with a lovely girl I would always fall in love with. The girls in our plays came from one of the many all-girl high schools in the area.

The directors, set designers, and choreographers were all students from Carnegie Mellon University which was right next door. Back then it was called Carnegie Tech and it was *the* theater school in the country. Still is; in fact, just today on Facebook, I see that six of its graduates are up for Tony Awards.

Senior High School Yearbook Photo

One day we were told that George Romero, a local filmmaker, would be coming in later in the week to audition some select students for a film he was about to make. I made sure I was selected and about 25 or 30 others auditioned. I had no idea who George Romero was but he was a movie-maker, and we all want to be in the movies right? I waited my turn, and back then, and for most of my life, even in the military, I wore glasses. But, I didn't want to wear them for this audition so I didn't. I got on stage and was handed the script pages and for the most part I could see the words for a while, but soon I stopped being able to make them out and stopped and put on my glasses. This got a huge laugh from George Romero and whoever he had brought with him. It turns out that I was just at the part of the script where there was some bad, coarse language, some swearing, and it looked like I couldn't believe what I was about to say and put on my glasses. This proved to be a happy accident because of all the students, he picked me to come to his office for a screen-test. I went, we did the test, but the movie never got made. It was to be called *Whine of The Fawn*.

Years later, when he was preparing to do *Night of the Living Dead*, I went down to that office again with my portfolio, and he remembered me. I told him I also do makeup and build props and he said, "I think we can use you on this thing," but you know the rest of that story. I went on to do nine movies with George Romero here in Pittsburgh, and one in Toronto. I owe my whole career to George. If there wasn't *Dawn of the Dead*, I wouldn't have had *Friday the 13th*, and that one-two punch is what launched me into my film career.

One of the most valuable things I learned at Central Catholic was typing. Three years of it. Today I amaze my daughter and grandson with how, without looking at the keyboard, I can type at high speed. I say valuable because, as you know, everything today is the keyboard.

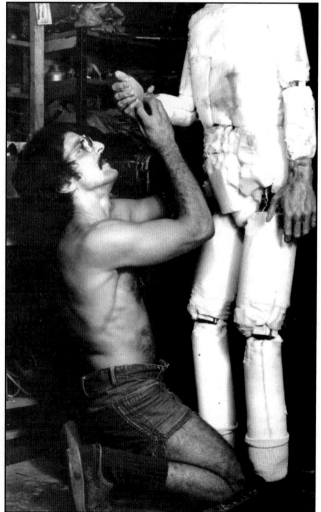

The Kennedy Assassination

I was a sophomore in 1963, and one day in Black Benny's class, an announcement came out of the P.A. speaker in the corner of the ceiling. President John F. Kennedy was shot and killed. Brother Benedict put his head in his hands on top of his desk and wept. So did a lot of us in the class. If you weren't there, you didn't know how Kennedy was loved: loved by the young minds in that class. We knew nothing about anything you read today about him, but I remember thinking at that moment, "Why would our government do something like that?" I wasn't a political scientist and didn't know much of what was going on back then, but I do know that was my first thought. Today I own just about every book written about the assassination, every video, and I am still pissed off that it happened.

What most people don't know or remember is that *Post*, a magazine like *Look* or *Life*, printed on its cover almost immediately following the assassination that "Three gunman shot at the President." *Ramparts* magazine at the time printed a separate small booklet called "In The Shadow of Dallas" and pointed out how many key witnesses died within a short period of time after the assassination. An actuary calculating the odds of such a thing came up with odds of over a hundred thousand trillion to one. Oh, don't get me started on the conspiracy. If that wasn't enough, there was a major motion picture that came out starring Burt Lancaster, Robert Ryan, and Will Geer that was about "Big Interests" deciding Kennedy had to die, and it showed how the assassins were hired and trained on moving targets in the desert before actually carrying it out. That movie disappeared from circulation. You can get the DVD today.

But like today, we have no idea what goes on behind closed doors and the more I read, the more it was likely that back then, things were covered up in the best interests of our country and its people. There could have been a major war over this event with Russia or Cuba, so this had to be quelled as soon as possible and it wasn't in our hands. It is one of the many things about history whose truth is not necessarily in the books, but in certain hearts and minds.

The Movies: Women

I wasn't just shy as a kid. I was pathologically shy, pathologically introverted. I hardly spoke. If a girl spoke to me, I was too paralyzed with fear to speak back and would just walk or run away. I didn't know the popular music of my day and couldn't talk about it. I didn't know cars nor was I interested, yet my schoolmates could look at headlights at night and tell me what kind of car was approaching and what year it was. I was only interested in monsters and makeup, and it seemed nobody else was. I pretended I was interested in such stuff, but after seeing the movie *Man of a Thousand Faces*, I was obsessed with makeup and creating monsters.

Susan Wright

Man of a Thousand Faces wasn't the only movie to have such a profound, life-changing effect on me. I think because of my cousin Vince I was able to hang out with some of his cool friends. You know, the ones that smoked and were confident with the girls and who saw me as kind of unique because I could change my face and become disfigured with makeup. I wasn't cool like them, but I remember a few years after my *Man of a Thousand Faces* epiphany when I went from being an obsessed kid to becoming a teenager, I saw *West Side Story*. Wow: that had a tremendous effect on me. I wore purple shirts and a wristband like Bernardo. Years later, my nickname in high school was Bernardo, but in my neighborhood with those cool guys, I was afraid to mention my interest in this movie musical that so impressed me. But one night I brought the album over to a party the "cool guys" were having and told them a little about the plot of this movie I loved about gangs in New York: it was like *Romeo and Juliet*. I put the album on their turntable and before long, after the snapping finger beginning number, we were all snapping our fingers, jumping on chairs and across the sofa, and being the Jets and the Sharks, and I felt totally responsible for introducing them to *West Side Story* and how great a musical could be.

Another movie that had a unique effect on me was *The Nutty Professor*, the Jerry Lewis one. In that movie I saw a shy, introverted, clumsy, "paralyzed with fear when a girl talked to him" guy who, after drinking a potion, turned into a cool, suave, confident lady killer named Buddy Love. After I saw that movie I put on my suit - I think I was fourteen - and took a streetcar to the college town of Oakland; I walked into a diner and became Buddy Love. I flirted with the waitress behind the counter and carried on conversations with the folks around me with a suave, confident,

Adrienne Barbeau

Zoe Bell

cool personality: my Buddy Love. So what's the difference here? I was still me, the pathologically introverted non-cool guy who, after seeing a movie, turned into my Mr. Hyde in the form of Buddy Love. To me, it means that stuff is inside us: in *The Nutty Professor*, all he needed was a potion, and all I needed was to just see that to realize that we all have a Mr. Hyde that we can release at will.

As you know by now, I went to an all-boys high school. We wore coats and ties every day and we were taught by Christian Brothers. I never dated in high school for a few reasons. I didn't have a car, I was poor, I had my big inferiority complex, and I thought I wasn't very good looking. Oh I tried... but not having a car was a huge disadvantage. If I did get interested in a girl, I would find out pretty soon how many other guys she was fucking and never me. So, I joined a lot of clubs and sports and got involved in the plays.

The girls in our plays came from some of the all-girls high schools in the area, schools like Sacred Heart or Ursuline Academy. There was this one girl, J——-, who was the most popular of all the girls and was always the lead in the plays and musicals we did and who never dated the same guy more than once. Those were her rules. She was a star. She was coveted by every guy there. She was THE Star and she deserved it. She was gorgeous and she was a really good actor. In fact, today she runs a theater and directs and acts there. Back then, she was really

something... and I was scared to death of her. This was an angel, an untouchable entity who was so far above me, so superior, so talented, that I only thought of her as ...as....well a superstar.

One day she actually spoke to me. By then I was doing the makeup in some of the plays at my school. She asked if I could design and perhaps teach her to do her Pinocchio makeup for something she was involved in and she invited me to her house. I was walking on clouds: clouds of immense fear and self-consciousness but I said yes and so I went to her house, her fabulous house. Back then, most of my classmates came from wealthy families, and their houses were all fabulous and made me feel even more inferior because we lived in such a poor, undecorated, four room row house. But her house was like a mansion I would see in movies.

She invited me down to her spacious game room that was as big as two or three rooms of my house put together, with a ping pong table, pool table, and a huge couch and television; we talked about her Pinocchio makeup. After a bit, I got up and started turning off some of the lights in the room. It just seemed too bright. She asked me what I was doing. I said I was just making it softer in the room. This had some sort of an effect on her toward me. She lit up and said she never thought that I had something like that in me...that I surprised her. I didn't fully understand it but I loved it: I had an effect on this heavenly creature...this coveted beauty.

42

We started dating. I became the only guy she dated more than once. We were a thing. I lost all of my best friends in school who couldn't figure out what the hell she was doing with me. I lost my very best friend Eddie who lived across the street because he was one of her "one date" guys...and I became Buddy Love again. She brought it out of me, or rather, she was the reason I released Buddy, and I loved what was coming out of me, including humor I didn't realize I possessed. We went to movies, dances, plays, and other high school concerts and it was this woman who chose the college I would go to and my major in journalism because soon, when she graduated, she would be heading off to college and to her, so should I.

About a year later, when she went off to college, I had an old, beat-up Plymouth something that was black, pink, orange, silver, and blue with those long tail fins, and I drove up to visit her. I remember pulling up to the dorm and she and her girlfriends were peering out a high window waving at me, and I could just see them commenting on her visiting boyfriend. I remember necking in my car and going to see the *Camelot* movie that was out then with Richard Harris and Franco Nero and feeling so inferior to Franco's great looks...but hey... I had J———-.

Shortly after I got home, I got the phone call from her that she met this football player, someone who just picked her out of the crowd and lifted her high in the air, and so of course, she had to fall in love with him.

Caroline Munro

Julie Newmar

Electra and Elise Avellan

Eiza Gonzalez

Margot Kidder

Caroline Williams

Julie Benz

Asia Argento

Brinke Stevens

Patti Tallman

Jennifer Rubin

Jodii Christianson

Ashley Laurence

44

A Brief Word About Being Married Three Times

I'm sure as soon as you hear someone has been married three times, you wonder what the hell is wrong with that person, but I have a good excuse for every one of them failing. My first marriage, well...Vietnam pretty much killed that one. I came home a non-feeling zombie. That happened to a lot of guys coming home from that experience. My second wife was my first wife's best friend. We failed at marriage after living together for four years. All

was fine before we got married, then, as she admitted over and over again, she took out all the hatred and pent up animosity she felt toward her father...on me. The marriage lasted six months. My third marriage, well I wasn't in love with her when we married. She was taking care of my dying father while I was away working, and when I came back, my father told me, "You should marry this one." She was pregnant and it was the right thing to do, but like she said five years later when we divorced, "I can't live in a house without love." I don't blame her. It was totally my fault. I deeply regret the lack of love I showed her. Out of that marriage came my totally amazing daughter, Lia.

Now I am married to the best thing that ever happened to me... my best friend and soulmate, Jodii.

My daughter Lia with Lizzy.

GOD

I was raised a Catholic with church every Sunday and every morning before our days in grade school, and the fear of mortal sin, and nuns and priests ruling our young lives, and prayers and rosaries, and Adam and Eve and the snake/Satan in the tree and so much else I see as just fairy tales today. I am not religious. My feeling is if one person is delusional, they call it insanity, but if a hell of a lot of people are delusional, they call it religion. I can't fathom this blindness toward the illogical and fantasy worlds that religion tries to brainwash into us. I sent my daughter and grandson to

> "I am not religious. My feeling is if one person is delusional, they call it insanity, but if a hell of a lot of people are delusional, they call it religion."

Catholic school for the sole purpose of exposing them to a great sense of morality that is a side effect of such teachings. However, I have to say I really miss the comfort and security that religion instilled in me for such a long period of my youth. The security of Heaven and eternal happiness and the belief that no matter how bad life can get, there is this hope of happiness later: I miss that. There is a hole in me where that was, that security. What has replaced that security? Do I believe in God? It depends on your definition of God.

Do you mean an intelligent force of nature that creates all things, or an egomaniac who lives in the sky and wants to be adored like an insane antique Roman dictator and says you can't eat meat on Friday?

If there is a God, presumably in control of everything, then I don't like him because of all the hideousness he allows to occur. If there isn't a God, then everything that occurs is happenstance and there is nothing we can do about it. I prefer to believe that what we call God is simply a force and from that intelligent force, everything comes to be, and though there are many individuals, there is only one mind, and we are all part of it, and that is why God is us and we are God. You can say God is in us, and that people are basically good, and everything that occurs is still happenstance, but out of this and us some really marvelous things exist in our world. You can't choose what comes at you but you can surely choose how you react to it. It's your choice and a lot of people don't realize that.

So...I've decided to only allow, as much as I can, the good things in life. Only the good stuff...good news...good movies...good people...good food...good reading...good Facebook posts. Really. I delete in a microsecond anyone who posts anything about abusing children or animals or horrific stuff that they think will call attention to themselves by exposing us to nastiness. They are deleted just as fast as I can touch the button.

How To Deal With Bullies

I learned how to deal with bullies early in life, like at the age of ten or so, and I learned how to deal with bullies, or rather practiced my theory, on the *Friday the 13th The Final Chapter* shoot.

When I was, I don't know...16, and I don't know why I did it, but after watching Marshal G...beat the shit out of someone at the local recreation center and bragging how he could break a brick in half with his fist and then actually doing it, we were hanging around and after another one of his boasts I said, "You're full of shit" I got just a look from him and then a smile, like "you don't deserve my attention." He was a big guy, nearly twice my size, and I admired his physique as I admired any physique after seeing Steve Reeves in *Hercules* about sixteen times. Then, after another one of his bragging jaunts, I said, "Oh why don't you just go home and lift some weights or something." I don't know whether I had a death wish or why I said it, but it seemed right. I know what it was. Everyone was afraid of him and agreeing with everything he was saying, and I just wanted to be different, something I always did in my youth. His reaction was a combination of "What did you say to me" and "How dare you say that to me," but he thought I was brave for saying it and actually said something like, "Hey...you're a spunky little kid." We became, or rather he

started treating me like, one of his best friends. I realized then that all you have to do is stand up to and defy a bully, and if you survive, you've made a friend.

On the *Friday the 13th* movie set, I was brought in as head of the makeup effects to replace someone they fired, and they had already started shooting. Ted White, the stunt man who played Jason, was fond of the previous makeup artist. Ted White was 62 at the time and was a really big, weather-faced cowboy of a guy who had doubled John Wayne and Charlton Heston, and chewed tobacco, and he hated being Jason and called him a freak. He was an abrupt, opinionated guy and did not suffer fools lightly, and he really didn't want to be a freak like Jason. I was explaining to him, in front of my crew, just how to hold onto the fake head of the victim's dummy we had created, so that he could twist it around after the saw blade cuts its throat. (I know... it's a living.) Ted got up angrily and said, "You know what? You take care of the makeup and I'll take care of the stunts," and he walked away.

I looked at my crew and the thought going through my head was something out of a self help book I

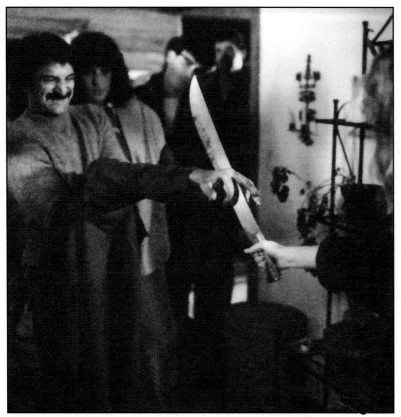

I just loved those stories, and he even taught me how to use a lasso by lassoing rearview mirrors on cars in the parking lot. The first time we put the makeup on him, in the studio just as a test, he made a suggestion as to how we could put the bald cap on him and I yelled, "Hey Ted, you do the stunts and we'll handle the makeup." He laughed and said he had that coming to him but that I didn't have to be an asshole about it.

We became fast friends and remain to this day. I mean it: to this day. I see Ted at conventions now and he is 92 and could still take on four or five guys and kick their asses. I am 70 and joke with him that I want to be like him when I grow up.

was reading about confronting whoever offends you and telling them it offends you, and I got up and took off after Ted. The crew jumped up and followed me and I confronted Ted in a hallway and said something like, "Hey Ted, when you said you'll take care of the stunts that offended me because I am a stunt man too." This was bravado coming out of me because I had done stunts in *Dawn of the Dead*, and *Martin* and staged the fights in *Heartstopper* and many more. He said, "I heard that about you." He was saying that and pointing his huge finger in my face, and my reflex action was to grab his finger and hold onto it as he was poking it at my face.

I looked at my crew and they were in shock as if they thought the very next thing that would happen was Ted's fist crashing into my face. Well, he started smiling and then we all started laughing at the scene in front of us. From that moment on, Ted would take me aside or walk with me and explain how various stunts were done in movies like car flips and high falls, and how he did various horse stunts for John Wayne and of course,

50

Vietnam

When I was nineteen, I enlisted in the Army. Yep, right in the middle of the Vietnam War. I enlisted to stay out of Vietnam and to support my then girlfriend who was pregnant and about to become my first wife. I was poor and the only way I was going to be able to support us was to join the Army.

When you enlisted you got your choice of Army schooling. When you were drafted, most likely you were going right into infantry and the front lines. I was already a photographer and had my own color darkroom in the basement of my house, so thinking, "What the hell would they need photogra-

phers for in Vietnam," I chose the Army School of Photography for my thirteen weeks of schooling after Basic Training. I enlisted on the hold program. This means that sometime within 140 days they would call you in. Of course that was when George Romero was gearing up for *Night of the Living Dead*. I followed him around his office, flipping pages of my portfolio as he scurried from place to place. He was a very busy man and said, "We could use you on this gig."

My girlfriend's parents had shipped her off to a home for unwed mothers in Baltimore to have our baby. When she came home, she avoided me for days and I had to track her down. I called up and questioned some of her friends, asking where the hell she was, and I found out she was going to a concert. I tracked her down coming out of the concert with some guy and that's when she told me she gave up the baby for adoption, and that her parents had made

her do it, AND I WENT NUTS. I became hysterical in public: I HAD JUST JOINED THE ARMY FOR US! It was just like the scene in *Scarecrow* with Gene Hackman and Al Pacino when his girlfriend gives up their baby. He went nuts in public and wound up sitting in a big fountain in the middle of town. I saw that movie many years later and identified with him, though I didn't wind up in a fountain. I did wind up on the ground, crying. She and her friend were able to calm me down and we agreed to meet the next day. We met and I said we needed to be married. I was this Italian Catholic and had gotten her pregnant, and it was just what I felt was the right thing to do. She did not have parent's approval and I was underage at 20, so we flew to Chicago and we were married in front of a woman magistrate in black robes and huge, round pink earrings.

After basic training, the Army photo school was located in New Jersey, so I could and did come home on a lot of weekends. When we were graduating, we went into this hangar to get our orders. One friend said, "Hey…look…I'm going to Italy. Another said, "I'm going to Germany" or "Hey, I'm going to Turkey." I said, "Hey, what does RVN mean?" "RVN! RVN! Oh man…you're going to Vietnam." I said, "Yeah, come on, very funny." "No man, that's Vietnam" was the collective reply from my friends.

On the Buddy System with Don Lawrance

52

In shock and denial, I went up to the Sergeant behind the desk. "Say... what does RVN mean?" He said, "Republic of Vietnam... NEXT." I walked away and made plans to die.

My wife moved to New Jersey to be with me for the 15 days notice I got before flying over to Vietnam. Once I left, she moved into my room at my parent's house. Going to Vietnam was like a scene from *The Deerhunter*. One minute, the characters are driving along American streets having a blast, drinking, going to a wedding, having fun with their friends and in the very next frame, WHAM— they are in Vietnam. I don't know whether it was the walking around in denial before I went, and then the sudden realization once I was there, but that scene in the movie is exactly what it was like. WHAM... I was there.

A strange thing happened when we landed there in a big Pan Am jet. I expected we all had to run for cover when this MP boarded the plane and greeted us wearing a chromed steel helmet and .45 automatics on both hips. But we left the plane calmly and could immediately feel the humidity like a big warm wet blanket attaching itself to our heads. For the entire year, it never left. It was beautiful: sunny and palm trees everywhere. It was like a tropical vacation land and we were all going on vacation. There was a large group of soldiers under a tarmac waiting to go home on the plane we came in on, and they were rude as hell, yelling things at us. "You pussies...you're here to take my place," and "You're going to die here, you faggots!" It seemed so unnecessary. They had just spent a year here and they were finally going home. I thought I would never do anything like that.

So I was in Vietnam for the next year. Back then, that was the tour of duty: one year. Let's sum up Vietnam: hot, sticky, humid, green, beautiful, primitive, best Asian food and marijuana I have ever and never had since, reconnaissance flights, helicopter flights, gun-toting, ammo-loading, photo-fluid, air-conditioned photo-processing vans, military intelligence troop movement,

beach lounge chair movie-watching with artillery blaring, cold water for the enlisted men, hot for the officers, angelic prostitutes, gonorrhea medication, photographing dead Vietcong bodies, American military equipment, small villages — some with Pepsi-Cola bottling plants, American car salesman in white suits staked out in the middle of nowhere in a PX selling soldiers cars that they would pay for monthly and pick up when they get back to the states, IF they got back... (Let me interrupt this summation by recalling what it was like when the grunts came in from the field of battle. The Grunts. They were the real soldiers. They were the ones out there confronting and fighting and shooting and dying. They were *Platoon*, and *Deerhunter*, and *Full Metal Jacket*. We, us military intelligence types in the 244 MI unit, were in a headquarters camp. Cafeteria, bathrooms, barracks. These grunts came in and I have to say I've never seen human beings like this. The human being part was not there. They were like free roaming animals. You looked into their eyes and they weren't there. What had they seen that changed them? What did they have to do to be alive? I often think of these men when I hear about post-traumatic stress syndrome.) Officers, USO shows, Jimmy Stewart visiting the injured men in our clinic, George E. Jessel's Star-Spangled Banner, bunkmates, shell casings hitting the tin barracks roof, friends, sports, tailor made shirts, bell bottom trousers and R and R.

That stood for REST AND RECUPERATION. You got to go on an all-expense paid week of rest and recuperation to Hawaii, or Australia, or

Japan, or Taiwan, after you were there for six months. I waited until my tenth month, because I didn't want to go back there and have six more months to go. I waited patiently until my tenth month and joined my then wife in Hawaii for seven days of paradise.

I got back to Vietnam with only two months left. Two months of feeling that if I was going to die, it would now happen in the next two months I have left. I was put on the worst duty possible (aside from being a grunt out there in the front lines where every stranger you see wants to kill you): Thirty Day Guard Duty. This simply means you are on the very perimeter of the camp, in a small bunker that holds four men, and out there in front of you is the jungle, and if they are coming, The Enemy...The Vietcong, the first people/soldiers they will encounter will be you.

Seven bunkers faced the tree-line. Each bunker was a sort of a wooden box surrounded by sandbags. Two floors: one was inside the box and on top of the box, there was a platform with sandbags all around that

54

could hold two men. Two men below stayed awake, and the guys above would sleep, and we took shifts.

Each little bunker was also an arsenal. We had a big M60 machine gun facing the jungle, grenade launchers, our MI6 rifles, and a Claymore mine. This was a rectangular plastic thing with steel balls placed against a block of plastic explosive. It would tear trees out of the ground or chop them in half, all within a 50-yard radius. The enemy used to come in and find them and turn them around towards us and then make themselves noticed so that if you hit the button to detonate it, it blew YOU away. We would paint the backs with luminous paint so as long as we saw it glowing out there we knew it was facing the right way.

The all-important thing was the trip flares, wires strung out in front of each bunker and on each side. If someone bumped them, they would shoot off a big bright flare so we can see who did it. They were spring-loaded so even if the wire were cut, it would still send off the flare.

Another incidental detail was, if you saw a hundred or a thousand VietCong coming at you from the jungle, YOU WERE NOT ALLOWED TO OPEN FIRE. You had to call the Command bunker, which was the very first bunker in the line, and report it to the officer there, who would come to your bunker with a night scope and if he saw the invading enemy, he had to call the battalion to report it and get permission to open fire.

Every weapon in the war zone was loaded with tracer rounds. Every third bullet. So if you were firing at night, you could see the tracer round, a red glowing speeding bullet, heading toward the target. When the Chinook helicopters went by and fired on

an area of the jungle, it fired so many rounds into the jungle— I think 600 a minute, maybe 6000— that from the rifle turrets of the helicopter would spring out a wall of red glowing light spraying across huge acreage. When that helicopter went by at three in the morning, we knew there was nothing out there any more that could do us harm. So, we could sleep better, or light up a joint and relax.

It was my seventh day of this guard duty, and the Chinook had just gone by, spreading a wall of red over the jungle in front of us, and me and Morales were down below, staring at the full moon. Like someone taking a surprise flash photo and sounding like a car backfiring, or worse yet, someone shooting at us, there was a sudden jolt in the peace of the night, a sudden shock when the trip flares right in front of our bunker went off, lighting the darkness, and I saw something moving quickly about fifty feet in front of us. I immediately grabbed the handles and trigger of the huge M60 machine gun and opened fire into the area. Morales unslung his M16 and started firing. The two guys who were asleep above woke up and immediately started firing and launching grenades, and someone set off the Claymore mine and wiped a clear path of vision through the foliage. Soon, every bunker in the line, all seven of them, was firing everything they had in front of my bunker. Forget your best Fourth of July celebration or the greatest fireworks you've ever seen: THIS was the loudest, brightest, most colorful,

that we covered every square inch of ground out there in front of my bunker with a bullet or some kind of grenade or claymore mine shrapnel, but I had to tell this general, "No sir." He said, "Well, next time, challenge it." All I could think of at that moment was this dialogue: Me - "Halt, who goes there?" The Duck - "Wannghhh...wannghhh...wannghh." The general quickly left in the caravan of jeeps, and I was promptly taken off guard duty. For the rest of my tour in Vietnam, my friends and even soldiers I didn't know called me "Duckslayer."

The next night we were attacked by Vietcong Sapper Squads. Sapper squads were Vietcong soldiers who wore nothing but shorts and carried bandoliers of grenades. They would pull the pin from the grenades after wrapping black electrical tape around the handles. Infiltrating the post, they would put these grenades in every gas tank they could find. The gas would eventually eat through the tape and the grenade would release its handle and go off. So you never really knew when a jeep, or truck, or a helicopter would explode. When they did, it was my job to photograph it.

When the Vietcong came in, there was a different kind of firefight at that bunker line I was in the night before, and men were killed. I wasn't there. I think the duck saved my life. As a result, I never eat duck.

Maybe this should be listed under the TIMES I NEARLY DIED OR WAS KILLED, but when we left Vietnam, and we are all sitting under that Tarmac watching the incoming soldiers disembark so we can board, we all did the same thing to them that we got when we landed. I don't know why, can't explain it, but we were hideously rude to them: calling them names and...I guess we felt so superior because we had been through it and they had not.... yet. Anyway, we got on the Jet, this huge Pan Am jet that held over two hundred soldiers. We were taking off and it was the first time in a year that I was sitting comfortably.

exhilarating, scary display you've ever seen. When we finally stopped...the duck that set off my trip flares flew harmlessly up and away against the night sky.

We could see a caravan of jeep headlights leaving the battalion headquarters and slithering along the road ...TO ME. The sounds of a gazillion rounds and explosions still echoed in the darkness. The lead jeep stopped, and out of the darkness, a figure approached me and I was scared. I watched this silhouette of a tall man come close to me, and as a trained soldier, my gaze was fixed on the shirt lapels of whoever was approaching me. If his rank was high I needed to salute this soldier. His shirt lapels entered my light and I saw the black emblems on his lapel. He was a general. I snapped into a clumsy salute pose, and all my attention was focused on his rank and I didn't look him in the face. He said, "Why did you open fire?" At that very moment, I lost the gift of speech. I think I sounded a lot like Daffy Duck doing convulsions with half words and sucking in breath and stuttering. The general said, "Calm down...calm down...what the hell happened?"

I was able to finally free the words "My trip flares went off." The general calmly said, "Hmmmmm... I guess I would have opened fire too. What was it?" "A duck sir." I feebly replied. The general asked, "Did you get it?" Now, I know

I put on the headphones and plugged them into the armrest and, I'll never forget, it was Classical Gas playing. We were finally going home, and I haven't heard music like this in a year. I cried. I was so embarrassed and I looked around and everyone was crying. All of a sudden the stewardess came running up the aisle screaming that the back door was open. What? We had just survived a year in Vietnam and we were taking off to go home AND THE FUCKING BACK DOOR OF THE JET WAS OPEN? Well, that was a jolt, and of course, after the door was closed, we all relaxed. We stopped in San Francisco before continuing on to our various home states and right then and there, I bought some casual clothes and took off my uniformandthrewitintothetrash.

When I got back home from Vietnam there was no fanfare, no hero's welcome returning from what was then a disgraceful scene. Look up the My Lai massacre. I was surprised to see some of my family there at the airport waiting to hug me: my brothers Joe, Henry, and Sullivan, and my sister. I burst into tears. I wasn't ready for that. To them, I had survived and that was to be celebrated. I just finished something that could have been much, much worse.

The next base I was assigned to was Fort Bragg in North Carolina and my life would change so much for the better there. I was just a soldier at first, living off base and going in for assembly in the morning, and that lasted about a week until a sergeant retired from a craft shop.

This particular "craft shop" on the base was where soldiers could come in and learn how to process and print their photos. There was a huge darkroom with booths filled with enlargers and chemical trays. I was

"We had just survived a year in Vietnam and we were taking off to go home AND THE FUCKING BACK DOOR OF THE JET WAS OPEN?"

given his position there and I no longer had to wear a uniform and no longer had to have a military haircut. I was basically a civilian, and every now and then I would have to put on the uniform and go to some officers' wives' party and photograph the goings on or photograph some award ceremony.

The craft shop is also where soldiers, mostly officers, would build remote control model airplanes that eventually they would fly. I would watch them spend months creating some beautiful, intricate fully mechanical plane and then take it out to the field and crash the shit out of it. I sat behind the cashier's desk mostly and sold model airplane parts and equipment. I would also go into the darkroom and load ten sheets of photo paper into small boxes that I sold at the cash register, and this is what would happen. It was usually an officer. Photo paper is light sensitive and that's why it has to be loaded in a darkroom. A customer would place it on a slab under the enlarger and project the film negative onto it, then put the paper into the three chemicals to produce a photo from a negative. I hope it's not too late to describe to you what film is. An officer would come in to print his photos and buy a box of ten sheets of paper, and while my back was turned putting his money into the cash register, he would open the box... IN THE LIGHT... and count the sheets. "Sir...you do know what makes a photograph right?" I could see and gloat when the realization hit him that light is what makes a photograph, and he just ruined the ten sheets he just bought.

"I would watch them spend months creating some beautiful, intricate fully mechanical plane and then take it out to the field and crash the shit out of it."

One of the greatest, most satisfying things that happened when I was "processing" out of the army a year and a half later was going from building to building gathering and signing various forms and just going through the process of leaving military service. I was in a play at the time playing Renfield in *Dracula*, the same stage play that Bela Lugosi had done so many times in his career. I had gone to the commanding officer of the base and showed him the photo in the newspaper of me and the cast of *Dracula* and asked if I could keep growing my hair for the part. He thought theater was wonderful and wrote me a note sayingineffect,"thissoldierisallowedtoappearashe appears" and my hair was getting really long. I was carrying that note in my uniform pocket as I was "processing" out when a huge master sergeant yelled at me to "GET OVER HERE SON." I went over to him and he kind of talk/yelled, like they all do, to get my ass RIGHT NOW to the barber shop and get a haircut and that I was a disgrace to all soldiers everywhere. With great unspoken glee I reached into my pocket and pulled out and showed him the note from my and his commanding officer. The look on his face: priceless.

The World Is A Stage

iving in Fayetteville, North Carolina was the happiest time of my life. But why? I was out of the Army; I wasn't working though I had a brief stint working for an advertising agency and now was living on unemployment and was as poor as can be. I had nothing but my little apartment... and my darkroom. That darkroom and my cameras saved me. I turned into a freelance photographer. My motto was "From Cheeseburgers To Politicians," and that's what I shot for the advertising agency, where I used to work, and other advertising agencies and for the local newspaper. I did weddings and well, cheeseburgers to politicians. But it was the happiest time of my life because of... THE THEATER. The Fayetteville Little Theater, which became the Cape Fear Regional Theater, and back on the army base, The Fort Bragg Playhouse. For the next eight years I was in a play nearly every night. I may have been poor as shit, but at night I was King Arthur, or Benjamin Franklin, or Henry David Thoreau, or Charlie Brown, or an ugly step-sister in *Cinderella*, or a drug addict in *Hatful of Rain*, or singing and dancing as Bernardo in *West Side Story*, or fencing as the fight captain in *Cyrano De Bergerac*, or Macduff in *Macbeth*, or Prince Philip in *The Lion In Winter* and many, many more. I was also doing all the makeup

Man of La Mancha

The Fantastiks

59

The Lion in Winter

in these shows. A typical evening was to show up early, do everyone's make-up, and in the case of *Fiddler on the Roof* that meant everyone's beard, do my own makeup, and perform the dances and stunts in that show. I was Littlechap in *Stop The World I Want To Get Off*, singing those incredibly hard lyrics: "Mumbo Jumbo rhubarb rhubarb jickety ju bob yak yak yak," and as King Arthur in *Camelot* singing, "How to Handle a Woman."

Camelot

I'm not a singer, but then neither was Richard Burton when he did it. I was a good Talk Singer. But the best thing that was going on was all the makeup I was doing, and I was doing it for the mirror and not necessarily for the stage. On stage you can get away with a lot because of the bright lights and the distance from the actors to the audience. You could overdo it and that is what stage makeup is. But...I did the makeup for the mirror. That means it had to be real in the mirror. The edges had to be invisible, and colors had to be real... and therefore

Camelot

60

involved in it: he would see what he could do. I got the call. A month later I was in Florida working on my first movie, *Deathdream*, assisting Alan Ormsby with the makeup effects. Because when I was in the right place at the right time— that bar where Forest Carpenter was sitting— I was ready. I had my portfolio ready to show him.

This led to my second movie with the same people, Bob Clark and Alan Ormsby, called *Deranged*. A few years went by afterward with no movies and lots more plays at the theater, but I realized if I wanted to take advantage of the G.I. Bill I was entitled to, I had to act soon as there was a seven year expiration on such a thing.

look very real on the stage, and this was great practice when later in my movie makeup career I had to make up faces that would be forty feet high and sixty feet wide on a movie screen. I photographed everything I did and created a portfolio which got me my first movie job, and later a full fellowship to Carnegie Mellon University.

I preach this to my students. Never go anywhere without your portfolio. Don't even go to 7-Eleven without your portfolio. Why? Because you never know when you are going to meet the person who can help or hire you.

I was delivering signs I had painted to a bar that had requested them, and I met this Indiana Jones type character sitting in the corner: Forest Carpenter. He wore a fedora and a leather jacket and we started talking, and he said he had been the art director on a movie that was shot in Florida called *Children Shouldn't Play With Dead Things*. This was one of Bob Clark's first pictures. (Bob Clark did *Porky's* and its sequels, *Black Christmas*, *Murder By Decree*, *A Christmas Story* and many more.) I mentioned I was involved in local theater and was also doing makeup. I had my portfolio in the car and grabbed it and showed my stage makeups to him, and he said they were gearing up to make another movie, and I should be

I decided to audition at Chapel Hill North Carolina for their theater program but I never heard back from them. My dad said I should audition in Pittsburgh somewhere and come home and live with him, so I thought of Carnegie Tech. That is what Carnegie Mellon University

Stop the World I Want to Get Off

61

Cactus Flower

Dracula

was called when I went to high school right next door. Carnegie Mellon University is THE theater school in the country. When I did high school plays, the directors, the choreographers, the set designers were all from Carnegie Tech. To me, back then, it would be an impossible dream to ever go there as it was so expensive, and I wanted to go there so badly having met so many great people who were going there and involved in our high school plays. So now, with the help of the G.I. Bill, maybe I would have a chance, and I decided to go home to audition there.

I did a scene I had memorized from when I played Chief Bromden from *One Flew Over the Cuckoo's Nest*. I know... I know... the Chief is a big dude like Will Sampson in the movie... but in the theater in North Carolina I played

Cactus Flower

him as a child... until he goes apeshit and destroys the place. I play apeshit well. Anyway, I did the audition and showed them my makeup portfolio. A month later I was doing a play back in North Carolina and got a letter from Carnegie Mellon University saying I had been accepted into the Acting/Directing program there, and that I would teach makeup on Tuesdays and Thursdays.

They had given me, based on my portfolio, a full fellowship. Fellowships are a fully paid scholarship usually given to graduates. I was the first undergraduate to ever get a fellowship from Carnegie Mellon University... because of my portfolio. AGAIN, I was in the right place at the right time and I was ready. THIS is why I tell my students to never go anywhere without your portfolio. There is no formula for success, but doing this sure helps.

Championship Season

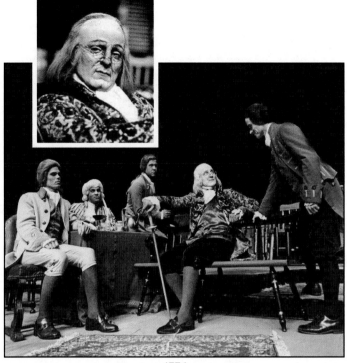

1776

Cyrano

Child's Play

One of the greatest actors of the 1800's: Tommaso Salvini

I can sum up my education at Carnegie Mellon by saying I learned more doing the seven years of live theater in North Carolina. Granted, there were some great classes, but I had already done all the things they were trying to teach us. I had already been in a war, did seven years of theater, and was ten years older than all my classmates who were mostly fresh out of high school. I was also doing a little movie work for George Romero on a film called *Martin*. I heard he was doing a vampire movie and I went down to audition for the vampire but he had already cast John Amplas, so I said I could finally (I didn't get to do effects in his *Night of the Living Dead*) do makeup effects for him in this movie, and I wound up doing that and playing a part and doing the stunts. It was great fun.

Godspell

Godspell

Hatful of Rain

Camelot

Black Comedy

You're A Good Man Charlie Brown

Deathtrap

65

Mid Back Flip in *Fiddler on the Roof*

Stop the World I Want to Get Off

West Side Story

Visiting that stage 43 years later

My annual dinner with my theatre friends to this day

The Horrible News

So, here I am, trying to live a happy life, liking people sometimes, except en masse when the herd mentality creates idiots, and every day, in every part of the world, over and over again the NEWS keeps telling us only how evil the world is and how many horrible things happened that day. We have a constant reminder that bad things happen all day, every day. We have well-dressed pseudo-journalists smiling as they tell us how many women were raped and children killed or abused, and they are smiling as they brag that they and their station are the first to bring you such disasters and tragedies.

I stopped watching the news years ago, and you know what? My attitude toward life has improved. My attitude toward people has improved. If you watch the news, and I agree with Michael Moore on the subject, you come away thinking black people are the scourge of the country, that all crime is committed by black people. Since I stopped watching the news, I am no longer a victim of induced prejudice. I've always felt that black people are sensitive, caring, happy people and my own black friends are judges, opera singers, scholars, philosophers, artists and just plain good people that I love to be around, and that is what I want my grandson to see and know.

The news socially hypnotizes people to belong to the club they are trying to create. They want you to be a member, and you don't have to join their club. You don't have to have its miserable message invade your life. They set up a story with real life villains and hope you keep watching to find out the latest development from an evil character they've introduced you to, someone that is perpetrating this evil in your lifetime in your world, and they like it even better if it's happening close to you.

Or worse yet, they try to make someone interesting to you by telling you over and over again what private little ditty occurred in their life. Who the fuck cares what Paris Hilton did today? Who the fuck cares what Jennifer Aniston, or Tom Cruise, or Jessica Simpson did today or any other day. But you can't turn your head without someone, some magazine, some TV show telling you. What's next? Jessica Simpson walked into a coffee shop and bought some coffee... OH NO!... and then came outside and got into her car and drove away. OH NO! What kind of coffee? Did she put cream in it? What was she wearing? What kind of car did she have?

I was a journalism major the first time I went to college, and I learned the mechanics and philosophy of journalism and took with me only a few basics. One was the meaning of communication: to send a message and make sure it's understood. This has helped me in many ways: in my life as a speaker and writer and as just a plain person trying not to be boring. I did very well at it and became president of the Creative Writing Club. The other important thing I learned, mostly from the club, was the meaning of the word "prosaic." What I remember about it is the importance of the way words are linked together, the sound they create, the mood created by a group of words together in a work, a story, a report. This is all in the interest of keeping it interesting. Part of that is to go in when you are done and eliminate all unnecessary words but keep the meaning. Journalism has had many important functions in life in the past in the hands of such thinkers as Edward R. Murrow and Cronkite and many more. It's sad to see such a degeneration of this science in today's world, and it pisses me off that I have to ignore most of it.

A Few of the Things That Are Wrong In Movies but We Accept It

et's start with this one: Our hero is in a gunfight and the bad guy is shooting at him and suddenly our hero runs out of bullets... and he throws his gun away? What? His gun. It's HIS gun! I've seen John Wayne do it, and even more recently, James Bond, Daniel Craig, does it in *Skyfall* on the train when he runs out of ammo. It's his Walther PPK, and he just throws it away. I can't believe he didn't raise a stink when the script said that or the director wanted it. This would not happen. It's your gun...I have to say it again...it's YOUR GUN! You would put it in your pocket or back in the holster until you got more bullets.

Another one: People are gathered in a room, you know, just sitting around, and for whatever plot reason, a rock bursts through the window with a note attached to it... and everyone makes a bee line to the rock to read the note. Are you kidding me? You would run to the window to see who the hell just threw a rock through your window. No... they have to read the note.

And more: The scene is people talking outside, in the country, on a city street, no matter where, and it starts raining— I mean a downpour— and they stand there and continue talking as if it is not raining and they are getting drenched to the bone. You and I both know that as soon as the first couple of drops fall, you are running for cover. I've seen people at the beach, after just coming out of the water soaking wet, or at a

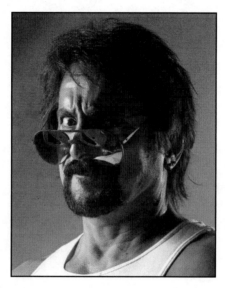

"No one ever says 'goodbye' when they finish a phone conversation."

water park where the idea of getting wet is why you are there, RUN for cover when it starts to rain. I always scream out loud at them, "Yeah...whatever you do...don't get wet at the beach!"

People never die realistically to me in a movie. Maybe on a rare occasion they do, but this is not something the average person would probably notice but they should. It's logical. When a person dies, all the muscles go slack. The arms and legs and head are limp and hang lifeless. This would also occur in the jaw muscles. I was a combat photographer in Vietnam and I've seen a lot of dead bodies and always... ALWAYS...the mouth is hanging open because there are no live muscles to hold it closed... YET... whenever someone dies in the movies, except on rare occasions like when Danny Trejo or Peter Coyote play dead in the movies... they hold their mouths closed so they look good to the camera. Not real... and again... not logical.

Ever been punched in the face? Really hurts doesn't it? If you're lucky it only happens once because it hurts so much right? Ever see a YouTube accidental punch in the face where the person hit is knocked out cold? That's what happens, and in worse cases, it's a severe head trauma and there could be brain damage. Hell, there are cases of boxers dying in the ring from a punch...a head trauma. Yet we fully accept that a

69

character in a movie can be bludgeoned on the head with a gun, or a club, and simply be knocked out for a little bit and get up and shake his head, and the little birdies circle around him and all is well. Or there is a fist-fight and it's John Wayne, or some similar monster of a big guy, and over and over again they punch the shit out of someone or someone is punching the shit out of them... over and over and over again and there is no head trauma?

And why is it that every time there's a car chase scene there has to be fruit stand nearby to smash through? And why, when people go shopping for groceries in movies, do they always come out with a long French bread and leafy lettuce that sticks out of the paper bag? And why always a PAPER bag?

Why when the cops enter an apartment where someone has just been murdered or raped do they investigate with flashlights? Why don't they switch on the lights? We accept all this.

"Whenever a cat appears, it has to meow endlessly... can't it just be quiet?"

On Having The Number One Makeup School

I used to do lectures/seminars at a couple of makeup schools or places that had a makeup program like the Art Institute which at one time, wanted to put my name on their program but like others, just never called back. The "others" were schools in California and Florida who would invite me in, I would do a seminar or a Q and A and I would make a few hundred dollars, and again they wanted to put my name on their program and move me to their state and pay my first six months rent and again, just never called back. This seemed to be a consistent trend. Some lawyer who had a warehouse or some prominent school would approach me about starting a school and then just never follow through.

So, when I got a call from Jeff Imbrescia about "starting a school," I wasn't too excited. To me, it was like "Oh another one." I was courteous and listened but really wasn't giving it too much thought. I would put off meetings or just plain ignore the messages about getting together to discuss it. But, he kept at it and even sent me a breakdown of what I would possibly earn if say... a hundred students showed up. I wasn't impressed but eventually accepted an invitation for lunch to discuss it. My opening comment to him was something like,

Nora Hewitt

Ryan Pintar

Jeff Imbrescia, CEO of Douglas Education Center

71

Danielle Noe

Morgan Hughes

Tyler Green

Wesley South

Daran Holt

Daran Holt

Ryan Pintar

"Yeah, I got your breakdown about how much I could earn, but Jeff, I spend more than that on cigars." He said something like, "Are you sure you are reading this right?" and corrected me on where I was misreading a decimal point. I signed with him that day.

The rest was him buying a building and us putting together a curriculum and sitting in front of the Board of Education, with his in-house lawyer Pat DeConcilis, to win approval of the idea. In short, he rolled the dice, followed through, DID call back, and really, earnestly went forward with creating the Tom Savini Special Makeup Effects Program at the Douglas School of Business. Later, when he created the Cosmetology program and Illustration and Graphic Art program, we had a meeting to change the name from the Douglas School of Business and I came up with the Douglas Education Center. He liked it and it stuck.

At this writing that was nineteen years ago and we are a raging success with students coming from

all over the world. It's a sixteen-month program with semesters starting in February, June, and October, and it's a degree program where students earn an Associate's in Specialized Business; more importantly, the students' attitude there is, "This is school?" because they are having so much fun making their dreams come true. Special makeup effects in itself has become a celebrity with shows like *Face Off* on the air and the movie magic potential students see in their favorite films. The list of my movie credits, and those of my teachers, is why potential students, who visit other schools, decide on mine.

At this writing my students have worked on movies like: *The Avengers, The Predator, Captain Marvel, Guardians of the Galaxy, Deadpool, The Conjuring, Annabelle,* Spielberg's *Lincoln, Pirates of the Caribbean, The Wolfman, Captain America, Inglourious Basterds, Teenage Mutant Ninja Turtles, X-Men, Superman Man of Steel, Star Trek Beyond.*

73

And TV shows like: *American Horror Story, The Walking Dead, Westworld, Mindhunter, Stranger Things, The Orville, Fear the Walking Dead, Z Nation, Preacher, From Dusktill Dawn.* Not to mention other venues like Prosthetic labs, Ocular Labs, Dental labs, Haunted Attractions, Museums, Theatre, Mask companies and Toy companies.

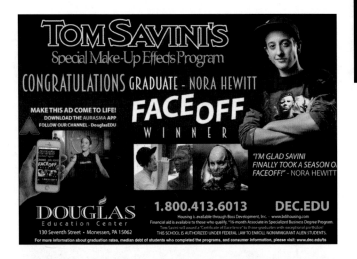

Google Says I Am A "Dick"

If you go to Google and type in my name, about the fourth entry is "Tom Savini is a Dick," or something like "Tom Savini Can Be a Douchebag to His Fans." I think I know how this happened but first I want to say I totally disagree, and by the responses from so many fans who have had very good experiences with me, mostly at the many conventions I do, they too disagree.

It's just not fair because I am so heavily influenced by how George Clooney behaved on the set of *From Dusk Til Dawn*. He was truly the nicest man I have ever met…to everyone! I was so very impressed with the way he made people feel. As I watched him, it was obvious it does not take a lot of special effort to be nice. He was a big influence on how I treat people when I am sitting behind a table at conventions.

Understand: you are trapped behind that table and anyone can come up to you and start a conversation, and sometimes it turns into an all-day interview, but for the fans, it is for them an opportunity to share with someone they've admired from a movie they've seen, or, in my case, some special effect or monster they've admired. My background in the theater instilled in me that each night the audience is new and for them it is a new show. Each person that walks up to my table…for them it is a new show. It is a performance. It is an exhausting performance. You may think… how hard is it to sit there and have people throw money at you all day? Ha! It's not that hard, but I smile at everyone, I look them right in their eyes and answer question after question and tell stories and anecdotes from the movies they love, and if they buy something, as soon as they hand over their cash, my hand reaches out to shake theirs. That makes them smile.

I do that with every single person, and at some shows that's hundreds of them. At one show I counted 750 fans that came to my table. At the end of the day, you are pretty tired of the performance, and though it is not hard physical labor, it is mental labor and you are exhausted.

So, here's how I think it happened, how I became a dick. It was in Texas at a convention and I was sitting there, happily signing and selling photos. There was a line and this lovely girl came up and chose a photo for me to sign. As I was signing it, my friend Rob, who was standing behind me, said "Hey…I am talking to Matt," and I said, "I don't want to talk to anyone right now." I signed her photo, and she gave me her money, walked about five feet away and angrily threw the photo back at me and walked off in a huff. We were stunned. Why the hell did she do that? Then we figured it out. What she experienced was me signing her photo and saying "I don't want to talk to anyone right now."

Well, we chased after her to give her some free photos and explain the misunderstanding but we couldn't find her. Later I learned she started a blog and a podcast about what a dick I am.

BEHIND THE SCENES AT THE FIELD INSTITUTE

OCTOBER 2003 / $3.95

www.wqed.org

PITTSBURGH

Why is this cat
so healthy?
See page 40

a
good
hard
look at the
pittsburgh
film biz

STAY
CONNECTED

WQED
Multimedia

0 74470 73000 2

10>

The Five Times I Almost Died or Was Killed

Vietnam

Well....just see my section on Vietnam. It's all there.

I Fell Asleep at The Wheel of My Car Going 60 Miles An Hour

I was returning home from Florida where I had just finished working on my first picture, *Deathdream*. I was driving my yellow Hillman Minx— just a used car I picked up in Fayetteville, North Carolina, where I was living at the time. It looked like an English cab and it was full of my luggage and props and makeup from filming. It was late at night, probably around three in the morning in Georgia and I was tired and just well.... fell asleep.

I woke up just seconds before hitting this huge metal pole. I saw it coming fast and had just enough time to turn the wheel hard to the left to attempt to get back on the road but the back passenger side of the car slammed into the pole and it spun me down the highway in the other lane and all over the place. The doors flew open and all my stuff exploded out of the car into the air and all over both sides of the highway. I can't recall right now how I stopped but I bet ya I blacked out. Passed out. That seems to be a recurring thing when I see something impossibly horrible about to happen to me. But I do recall backtracking down the highway and collecting my stuff off the road and in the woods and having to tape the back door shut on the side that hit the pole. I was lucky there was no traffic coming at me or behind me. I was wide-awake for the whole rest of the ride back to North Carolina, and I have never fallen asleep at the wheel since.

I Fell Off A Hundred Foot Cliff

Around 1967, I was president of the Point Park University Explorer's Club and on a rock climbing excursion at Cooper's Rock in West Virginia. Cooper's Rock is a hundred foot rock face with a plateau on the top that we would climb and then rappel back down to the bottom, but first we had to climb it.

When you climb a rock face with associates and you are ahead of them, you are all connected by the same rope attached to you by a crotch harness. As you climb, you pound pitons into the rock with a small hammer. You have to listen to the sound of the piton being hammered in. It must make a higher pitched twang with each hit or it isn't in solid. Pitons are metal spikes with loops at the end and in those loops you clip a D-ring. You've seen those before: they are metal rings that look like the letter 'D," and one side is on a hinge that you can push in to clip

77

things inside. When you close that side you can screw it into the rest of the ring so it locks solid. The reason for all this is when you pound in your piton and attach the D-ring, you also pass your rope through the D-ring and continue climbing. This way if you fall, in theory, you only fall as far as the D-ring attached to the rock face below you. When the climber below you comes to your D-ring, he simply pulls the rope out of it until he passes it and re-attaches it to the rope behind him. Get it? The nylon climbing rope is supposed to hold the weight of a truck as long as the rope isn't damaged or dirty.

I was the lead climber and I was almost to the top and came to an overhang. An overhang is a section that is not flat like a wall but juts out over and above you like a ceiling. I was making my way along it like a fly on that ceiling and I started to lose my grip; I couldn't see how I could hang on and called to the guy below me that I couldn't hang on and was going to jump. He braced himself against the rock face at the D-ring about thirty feet below me and said, "Don't jump! Make your way along until you just sort of can't hang on any more." That's what I did, and this is how I know my mind and body will take care of me in a traumatic situation and just make me black out, or pass out.

I kept going until I felt my hands letting go. I was a hundred feet from the forest floor above the trees and sharp jutting rocks I had passed on my climb upwards. I wasn't looking down, and if I let go, I would plunge backwards into the unknown. I saw my hands let go of anything that was holding me against the rock face. The next thing I knew, I was jolted into consciousness by the sudden stop of the rope catching my falling force. I fell around sixty feet: the thirty feet between me and the D-ring and the thirty feet when I passed it. I was now about thirty feet *below* the climber who used to be below me, swinging in mid air from a rope attached to my crotch harness.

I didn't experience the fall. My mind protected me from that trauma when I blacked out. It could have been a different experience if I had hit something within that sixty-foot fall.

Just recently, a month ago in fact, I had a head-on collision into the back of stopped car. There was nothing I could do: that's why they call them accidents and why accidents are so scary. There is nothing you can do. I was behind a truck and decided to pass it and when I pulled into the passing lane and that line of traffic was at a dead stop. I slammed on the brakes with both feet but I wasn't going to stop and was headed fast right at the car in front of me. I couldn't believe what was going to happen: again, it was a plunge into the unknown, and I must have blacked out and the collision woke me up. My sunglasses were broken and a huge gouge was scraped across the lenses; the pants at my right knee were torn and my knee was scraped. I don't know how. I didn't experience it. My feeling is that I went limp and that's what saved me from more harm. Consciously going limp saved me from my next date with death.

My Trampoline Accident

The trampoline accident had to have been seen to be believed. If you were looking at it, you would say, "well, that person is dead, or in a wheelchair... or beheaded." I did send it to *America's Funniest Videos* and I heard back from them. They thought it was too terrible and not funny.

Suffice it to say, I was practicing back flips, and oh yes: this wasn't a trampoline like 14-feet wide with a huge bouncing surface. This was a "mini-tramp." A mini-tramp is what gymnasts and stuntmen use. It's about three feet square, and the bouncing surface is about a foot and a half square situated in the middle of a metal frame at an angle to you. You run at it and bounce/jump on the bouncing surface and it either hurtles you forward— ideal for poolside and diving, flipping into the water, or forward flipping into the air and landing on the ground— or backward so you can do a back flip and land on the ground, or gym floor ideally.

It was winter and I set my mini-tramp up in the backyard on the hard, cold ground. I usually set up a video camera so I can check my height and form. I was alone. I did a number of runs and jumps on the mini-tramp and successful back flips onto the ground. I was getting a lot of height when I checked the video, so that's what I decided to work on. My height was getting better when this fucking dog next door started barking at me. It ruined my concentration.

You can see it aggravating me on the tape. I started taking more time between back flips, and the jump right before the accident I didn't flip at all: I just bounced off the mini-tramp and stiff-legged landed on the ground standing like before. Then I ran to the mini-tramp, jumped on the bouncing surface, and flew high in the air; my body did a small arc and I landed backward— right on my head.

You know.... a funny thing happens right before you think you're going to die. Life goes in slow motion. It happened to me before I drove the motorcycle through a store window in *Dawn of the Dead*. The effects guys poured this huge slab of breakaway glass on the shopping mall floor, and when it dried, it was lifted up and it became the store window I would drive through. They poured it too thick, however. For years afterward, George Romero would pull out this huge chunk of the window and say, "This is the breakaway glass those guys made." He would pound on his desk with it, causing no damage to the glass. As I drove toward it on the motorcycle, suddenly, it was as if I was in slow motion. I had never done anything like this before and I guess it was... that the unknown was about to happen to me. It's a strange feeling. On film, it happens very quickly, but in my mind I was observing people watching me as I approached the window. The tires weren't spinning really fast and like in a dream, I was traveling kind of

slow to the impact, and I was able to think out what I was going to do: *Let's see: I'll hit that window and it will break and I'll fall backward off the bike but I better angle the bike to the left after the hit so when my body leaves the bike it will fall to the left and hopefully slide on the ground and someone can stop it instead of it driving into people.*

I actually had time to think of all this. Same thing happened as my body left the mini-tramp. It happens very fast on the tape but in my mind I went into slow motion. *Let's see... I guess I'm not going to flip backward onto my feet by throwing my head*

Our neighborhood pool.

back causing my body to follow suit because I'm still looking forward. But my body is flying into the air and the momentum is causing my feet to rise up way in front of me. Hey... the top of my head is heading straight into and toward the ground. I better not tense up because that could really hurt on the hard frozen ground, so I better relax and just let things happen. I think that is why at the last second, my head sort of turned toward my chin and I came down hard on the back of my neck and head.

I immediately ran into the house. Good sign huh? I didn't break my neck and I won't be in a wheel chair. I grabbed a bag of ice (I don't know why we had a plastic bag filled with ice right then) and put it on my neck. A day or two later I couldn't move my head to the left without getting dizzy. In Dr. Nicotero's office later, after a barium injection, I could watch the flow of barium and blood on the x-ray machine flow up my artery and into my head. When I turned my head to the left, the flow stopped. Aha!

Drowning in the Neighborhood Pool

I was around five years old and my poor sister, stuck again with babysitting me, brought me to the very crowded neighborhood swimming pool. I was sitting on the edge of the four-foot deep section, and I guess someone dove into the pool over me and knocked me in. I didn't know how to swim, and I instantly sank to the bottom and stood up. I was standing on the bottom not knowing what to do or how to get out of the water, and I was only about three feet tall. All I could do was raise my hand out of the water and wave hoping someone would see my hand. I was running out of air after not having a chance to take a breath before being knocked in. I must have blacked out just before someone grabbed me out because I remember dreaming. There were stars and I was wondering what I was doing in space among all these stars and if I was awake or dreaming. Suddenly, it got very bright and noisy and wet as I came to, lying on the concrete of the pool along the water, surrounded by people yelling and my sister was crying. I'm sure she caught hell at home: even more than when she ran over my head with her bike.

There have been many other traumatic things that happened to me, like getting accidentally stabbed in my side by a switchblade in the middle of a performance of *Zoo Story*, or my sister running over my head with her huge bicycle when I was around two years old (giving me a concussion), or my ex-wife stabbing me in the throat while we were fencing without protective masks, or rough-housing with a girlfriend who had a serrated kitchen knife in her hand and getting my finger cut off, or the hand grenade in basic training. THE GRENADE! I FORGOT ABOUT THE HAND GRENADE!

The Hand Grenade

Part of the training you get in the Army during basic training is how to throw a hand grenade. They lead you into this tall maze of sandbags and you hear these really loud explosions from soldiers in front of you, throwing hand grenades into this open field. Everyone is nervous, and drill sergeants are screaming at you, and you slowly make your way through the maze until you come to the opening and there is this really badass sergeant with scars on his face, wearing a steel helmet.

He didn't talk to you but he yelled his instructions. "DON'T YOU EVER THROW A HAND GRENADE LIKE YOU SEE THOSE PUSSIES DO IT IN THE MOVIES. YOU DO NOT, I REPEAT, YOU DO NOT STIFF ARM LOB IT OVER YOUR HEAD. YOU THROW A HAND GRENADE LIKE YOU ARE THROWING A BASEBALL: AS HARD AND AS FAR AS YOU CAN THROW IT. YOU WIND UP LIKE A PITCHER AND THROW IT LIKE YOU ARE TRYING TO STRIKE OUT A BATTER. I AM GOING TO HOLD THE GRENADE WITH YOU, MY HANDS OVER YOURS, AND PULL OUT THE PIN WITH YOU. THEN I WANT YOU TO THROW IT AS FAR AS YOU CAN. DO YOU UNDERSTAND?" "Yes, Sergeant," I muttered.

He pulled the pin out and I don't know what happened. I must have gone into reflex movie mode or something because there I am, holding this live grenade in my hand, and like Audie Murphy or John Wayne or any number of movie soldiers I've seen throw grenades, I stiff arm lobbed it over my head and it did a small arch and landed just on the other side of small two foot wall of sandbags.... about six feet from us.

The sergeant went crazy on me, and I don't blame him. He knocked me to the ground and after the grenade went off and sand and bits of sandbag had settled on us, and he took off his steel helmet and started beating me with it, yelling, YOU TRYING TO KILL ME BOY?! YOU TRYING TO KILL US?! GET THE FUCK OUT OF HERE, SOLDIER! Well, this isn't really on my list of how I was almost killed or died.... but it's pretty close.

Gun Control

There is a bad side and there is a good side. I don't believe automatic weapons, machine guns in essence, except in movies like below, should be owned by the general public. I can pay a fee and fire them at a range if I wanted to. My handgun? When you're cowering behind me in a school, a supermarket, or a theater because some suicidal mental deviant just blew someone's brains out of their head onto a wall, and when he shoots random people, killing them instantly in a waterfall of blood, and screaming, and tears, and prayers, and when you're cowering behind me because I have a gun and the deviant has spotted you and is heading your way, and when I shoot him in the head, downing him instantly and preventing you from becoming one of the bleeding dead...you will LOVE my gun. You know it, and I know it.

What happens on the streets somewhere every day is the loathsome, unspeakable, disgusting, repulsive, helpless tragedy when mental deviants or socially evil people use a weapon, and that is the bad side to gun control. The scenario I just described above that saves your life and others: that is the good side. This is the state of things in our country.

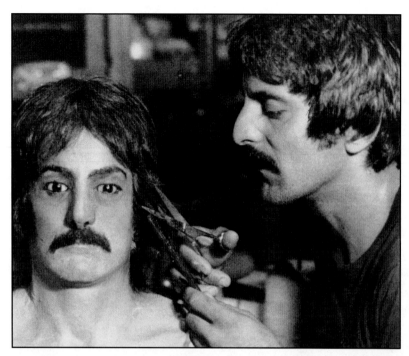

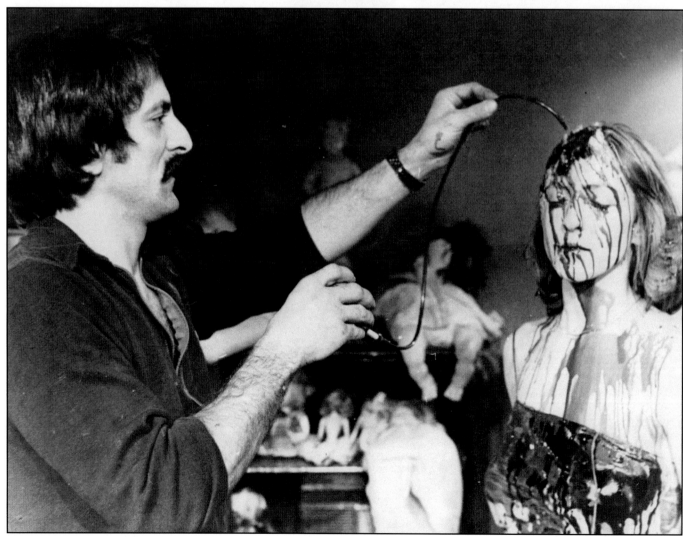

I Smoked A Joint with Timothy Leary

I was at a convention in New York. I don't remember where — back then is all a blur — but probably the old Roosevelt Hotel across from Madison Square Garden. I do remember Forrest Ackerman was there, and back then, he was a common occurrence at a horror convention. I was sitting in the green room relaxing, and Timothy Leary (if you don't quite know the impor-tance of this, look him up) was sitting on a couch all by himself smoking a joint. He took a long hit then looked around for someone to hand it to. I leaped over furniture and crawled across that couch to get to him and grab the next hit off that joint so that I could say, and tell you now... I smoked a joint with Timothy Leary.

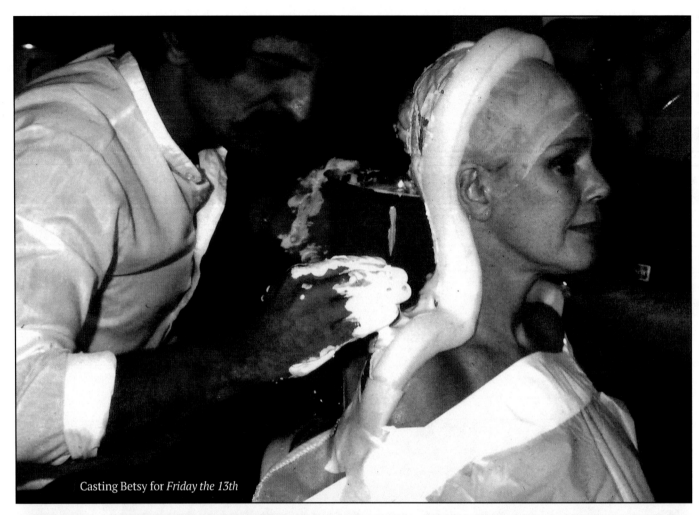

Casting Betsy for *Friday the 13th*

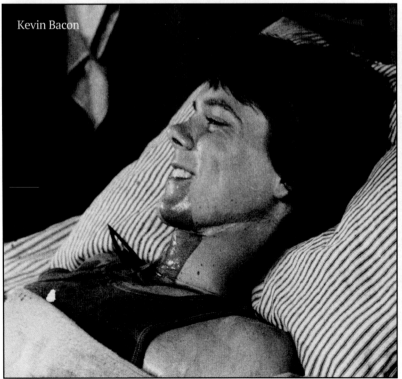

Kevin Bacon

Jeannine Taylor

My Internet Date Nightmare

I got an email from A...... saying she was big fan of mine and she would like to give me her virginity. She included some photos, I thought she was really attractive, and we exchanged phone numbers and started talking; she seemed like a very sensitive person who had some family issues. I was just getting over a bad relationship, and in those days, I was open to suggestions like she was offering. I flew her in from New York, and she spent a few days with me, helping me set up my home gym, alphabetizing my video collection, and going along for the ride to look at a possible location for Terrormania, and I took her up on her offer, and it was very nice. One late afternoon, I got a voicemail from a friend who said, "Tom... TOM... the world is ending... watch the news... IT'S ALL OVER!" I turned on the tv and saw jumbo jets flying into the World Trade Center. I had to get A...... back to New York, but no planes were allowed to take off. I was able to get her on a bus, and she was able to get home during this abominable catastrophe.

Later, actually a few days later, when I, like so many, came out of my shock and was able to function a little better, I decided to lose myself in a movie or two. I went to my video collection, which is on floor-to-ceiling shelves left over from the set of the movie *Creepshow*, happy to have everything newly alphabetized. I noticed that every movie I have ever worked on as an actor or that I did the special makeup effects for— including some rare ones that you can't even get any more— were gone. The boxes were empty. Get it?

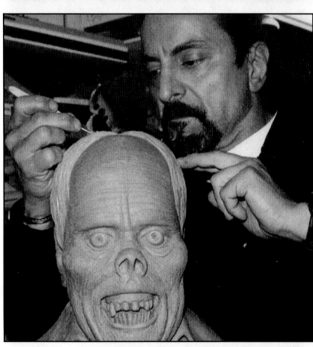

My Encounter with The Paranormal

irst of all, I don't believe in this crap, and I really despise those cheap TV shows about the paranormal where the whole show seems to be about "What the hell was that?" They say it in every commercial and it seems THAT is the climax of the show, somebody saying that and that is all it's about. But this really happened, and it scared me, and I have no explanation other than there might really be something out there.

Before I did *Tom Savini's Terrormania*, a haunted attraction which ran for eight years that I created and Jeff Imbrescia, the president of my school, financed, we were looking at possible locations. Eventually we settled on an abandoned K-Mart very near the school and it was spectacular: 27 rooms with a cemetery, a subway, a swamp, and caves... it really was the best haunted attraction ever, but that is another story.

When we were searching for a location, Jeff called me and said his real estate agent has a place in mind not too far away from the school and it has lots of parking space, an old barn, and a big house, and the owners want to sell it. BUT... it might be haunted. The owners really want to get out of the house and move to Florida. The previous owners only lasted a week there, and before that, the owners never made it past the driveway before they sold it. The current owners have only been there around two months. We made plans to go there on one condition. We were not to say anything about looking for a place to build a haunted attraction and we were not to say anything about their place being haunted.

So the plan was to go there and pretend I was looking to buy a house and Jeff and the real estate lady were helping me. It was Jeff, the real estate lady, me, and A......., my "internet date from hell." When we arrived there, the real estate lady told us the house

was over a hundred years old and part of the underground railroad to help slaves escape the South. The original owners and family were buried in a cemetery that was right there on the land, next to a barn that was slightly leaning to the left and the dilapidation of the doors and upper windows made it look like a big, brown, sad face. There was an empty swimming pool and the inner walls were all chopped up from a huge deer that had wandered into the empty pool and couldn't get out so it had rammed its antlers into the sides.

We went inside the house to meet the couple who owned the place and they really looked stressed, and tired, and jumpy. They were the only people home. They had photos of Florida all over the kitchen walls and on magnets on the refrigerator and a Florida license plate on the table on top of maps of Florida. These people really wanted to go to Florida. They gave us a tour of the house upstairs and showed us trapdoors in the floor of some of the closets leading to stairways, and this was part of the underground railroad. Halfway through the tour, we stopped back at the kitchen and for some reason, Jeff asked if there was an aerial view of the land. They said yes and pulled out the photos. While they looked at the photos, this very beautiful, classical piano music from somewhere in the house started playing. I looked at A........ and she looked back with a "hmm...that could be spooky" look. I guess we both thought at the same time how creepy and fitting it was: it was as if this was a scene in a movie about fooling some people into selling their house in order to make it a haunted attraction.

The tour continued and soon we were entering a large room. As the door into the room opened, I could see a tile floor and a fireplace on one wall and the end of a grand piano. As I continued to enter, I fully expected to see someone sitting there at the piano who had just played that beautiful music we heard. But there was no one sitting there and the tour continued. We met back at the kitchen and told the couple what a lovely place it was and that we would get back to them.

In the car, as we drove back to the real estate agent's office, we talked about many things in the house, and I said, "How about that beautiful music that was playing...wasn't that a little creepy?" and Jeff and the real estate lady said, "What music...we didn't hear any music." I thought they were kidding and said something like, "yeah right," but they genuinely did not hear the music. Now we seemed like we were trying to pull something on them... like we were trying to convince them the place was haunted because we heard music and they didn't. They were really making fun of us trying to pull something so immature and dumb on them like hearing beautiful classical piano music, and we were like, "NO NO... we really heard this wonderful live piano music while you were looking at the aerial photos." To this day, Jeff swears he did not hear any music and it makes me think we wasted a perfect opportunity. I wonder if we had said at the moment we heard that music in that kitchen something like "Hey...wow...what beautiful music... who is playing that?" what kind of reaction we would get from that couple. Like... maybe a look of shock with them saying, "Oh my god...you hear it too?" Perhaps they had been hearing that music all along and it was scaring them and driving them crazy for Florida. What would Jeff and the real estate lady have said... AT THAT MOMENT? We'll never know. It's a missed opportunity. We heard that music. Who played it?

Dreams

f I were a casual observer of life here, like let's say an alien race from a different planet observing us, you might hear me say, as I observe us, that this is a culture that at night, when they dream, they create a life just as real as the one they live every day, with objects just as real and solid as they experience in their waking lives... except in dreams, they can do fantastical things like fly or jump, cut to different places and people, or be chased by monsters or face their fears and nightmares. They can do anything or go anywhere their thoughts take them because their thoughts create a world just as real to them, and yet the absurdity of the situations in their dreams doesn't dawn on them or seem absurd or unreal no matter how different and silly or illogical it seems to them. They live it and react to it just as they do in their waking lives.

Why then doesn't it occur to people that the thought or intelligence that creates their everyday waking life (some call it God) is the same as their thoughts creating their dreams. In their dreams, they are not just plunked into a situation, plunked into a setting, or plunked like into a movie set or a staged scenario: they are not placed into a setting.... THEY CREATE the setting, no matter how elaborate or full of detail... a city, a mad laboratory, a library, a mansion full of elaborate furniture... everything they encounter was created by them, thought up by them. And the mere thinking up of all these things creates them as solid and as real as in life. So again, why doesn't it occur them that they are as close as they can be to being "God" or the intelligence that creates all things? They are doing it, they are creating life as solid and real as can be sensed by their senses, yet they don't realize that in their dreams

they are seeing without using their eyes: their eyes are lying in bed with them closed as they are unconscious. They are hearing sounds that don't exist. Don't forget they are lying in a room where those sounds are not occurring, and they are touching solid objects, and smelling the smells, and tasting the food THAT DOESN'T EXIST EXCEPT WITHIN THE WORLD THEY ARE CREATING, just as they do in the life that something else, someone else is creating? No. Shouldn't that say to them that there is one mind and they are all a part of it and it is exemplified when they dream and do the same thing? Yet, it is treated with indifference and not even thought of as something so overwhelmingly extraordinary, but rather as common an occurrence as a sneeze, or a nap, or indigestion: something "ordinary."

This would have to upset and confuse and baffle the observer that something so remarkable, so fantastic and supernatural, is occurring to these beings and they are not even seeing the connection between themselves and the "God" they are saying is in charge of everything, creating everything. They are not seeing the truth: that "God" is within them. It is also amazing that they don't get the correlation that when they wake up from a dream it seems they are programmed to forget the dream as soon as possible. There are many cultures that believe in reincarnation. So, the correlation between waking up from a dream and instantly forgetting it can be the same thing that happens when you are reincarnated after death. You are programmed to forget what came before. Row, Row, Row your boat: life is but a dream.

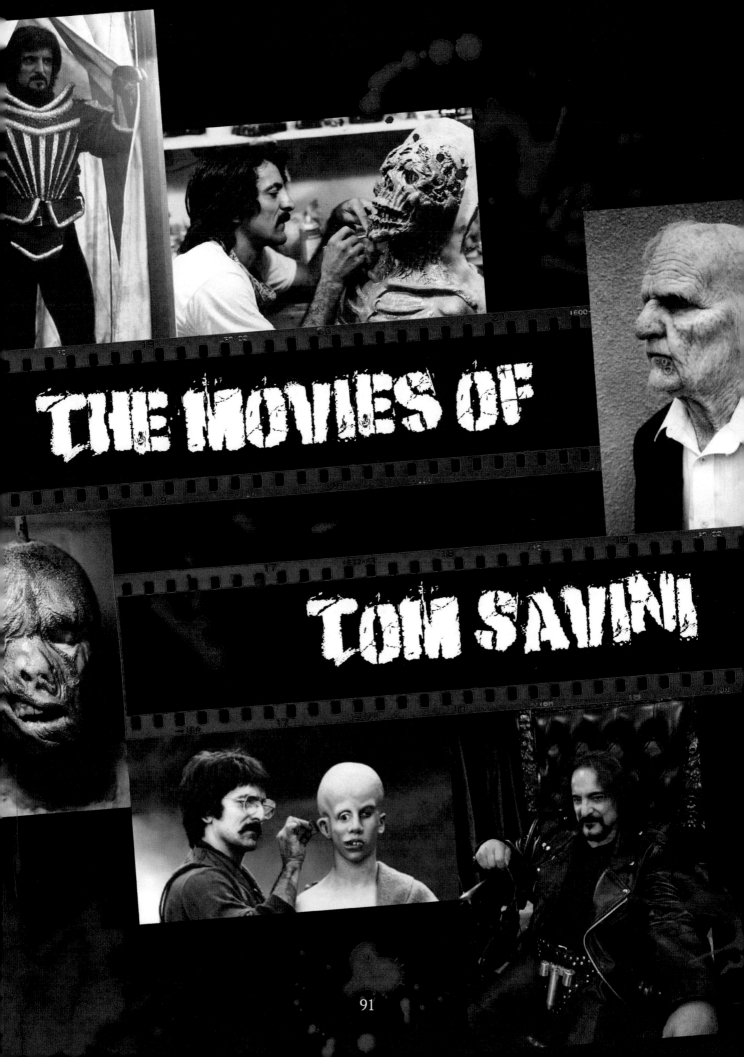

THE MOVIES OF
TOM SAVINI

From creating Jason Voorhees to killing him. From killing vampires to being one. From stunts, to effects and acting, Tom has had a career that has lasted over fifty years in the film industry, a feat in of itself. In addition to having an amazing career, he has inspired new filmmakers, scared millions more, and graced the screen alongside Hollywood royalty. A boy who grew up fascinated by movies, loving them, idolizing the stars, yet never dreaming of working in movies, Tom is now part of Hollywood's history.

While the industry knew his name and sought him out, fans only saw his amazing work, not knowing who he was until *Fangoria* magazine started in 1979. The first issue did a feature article on Tom and his makeup effects in *Dawn of the Dead*, introducing the world of future "fan boys" to the man behind these spectacular effects. As *Fangoria* grew in popularity and Tom did more and more movies, the fans eagerly started to anticipate a film that "Savini" did. While Tom was just one aspect of a film, people started to flock to movies just because *Savini* worked on them, knowing the effects would blow their minds. Some films even started to put his name on advertisements to bring in this new fan base.

As Tom started to become the rock star of makeup, it wasn't long before the national media took notice. Instead of the film's stars doing promotions for the movie, Tom was now doing interviews to promote the release of new films. He even became a regular on *Late Night with David Letterman*. He appeared five times throughout the decade, each time annoying and amazing David

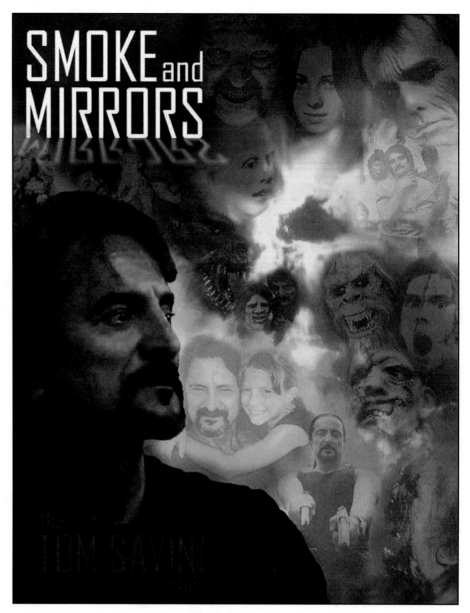

by showing him how he created effects for a new movie he was working on. Appearing on this show, lighting David on fire, shooting him in the head and grossing the host out made Tom known to an audience beyond that of just the horror fans; he was now known by the general public.

With so many movies under his belt, it is hard to document all of them in detail. What follows is a highlight of his career that focuses on select stories from some of his more memorable movies.

Dawn of the Dead is still known as one of the greatest, if not the greatest, zombie films of all time. From Tom's legendary zombie effects and creation of a partial decapitation by helicopter, to the effects master's stunts and acting in the film, the film is overflowing with Tom's talent and passion. With countless articles, books, and even documentaries made on the film, pretty much everything that can be known about the film is out there. Therefore, instead of rehashing what is known, here is a something about the film that Tom has never really shared: at the time, Tom was *obsessed* with Darth Vader.

Star Wars had come out the year before they started filming, and Tom instantly fell in love with the villain. He simply HAD to be Darth Vader that Halloween. Alas, *Star Wars* merchandising hadn't yet reached the frenzy it later became. Tom tried to get a Darth Vader helmet/mask from Don Post but was told, "Oh yes, we can get that for you *next* August." That wasn't going to work, obviously, so Tom built his own Darth Vader.

The costume wouldn't be a big deal but the mask and helmet were going to make or break it. He used the steel helmet he wore in the Army and built it up with auto body filler. It weighed a ton. He sculpted the front of the mask out of clay, then made a mold of it, poured foam rubber into the mold, and dug out the foam until his head fit. That Halloween, he WAS Darth Vader.

He and his friends entered a Halloween contest and a beautiful judge, Jeanie Jeffries, selected Tom as the winner. Tom took off his helmet and it was love at first sight. He hired Jeanie as his assistant on *Dawn*. She also played the "Blonde Zombie" who is shot from behind, sending parts of her face onto Scotty before she is kicked out of the truck. Tom donned a blonde wig and did that stunt as well.

While this might not be a tale about *Dawn of the Dead*, in Tom's memory, the two things are intertwined and inseparable.

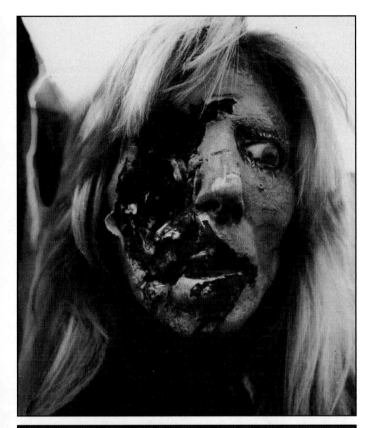

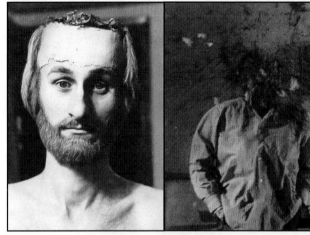

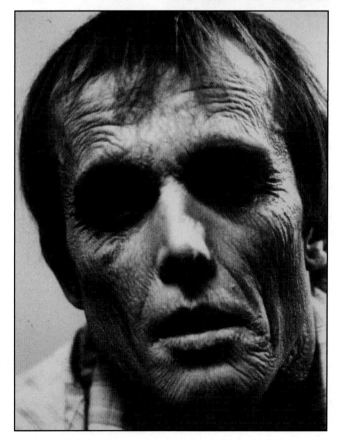

Once again playing a small role in addition to doing the effects, Tom started work on *Maniac* in early 1980. During their first meetings, Tom found himself telling Joe Spinell over and over again, "No, you are not cutting *that* off a woman." Joe seemed to want to take the film in a direction that was bit too dark, even for a horror film.

The filming went well and Tom did some more amazing effects, his favorite being...killing himself. Tom's character,

dubbed Disco Boy, was to be killed in a car. Not only did Tom have to make a dummy version of himself, he was also going to be the one doing the killing by blowing off his own head. With the dummy of Tom behind the wheel of the car, Tom dressed as the killer, crouched on the hood of the car, and fired both barrels of a shotgun through the windshield, splattering his head all over the car. Tom only had one shot at the effect and pulled it off just right, killing himself for the first time.

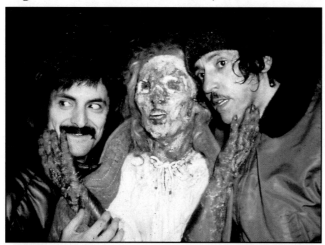

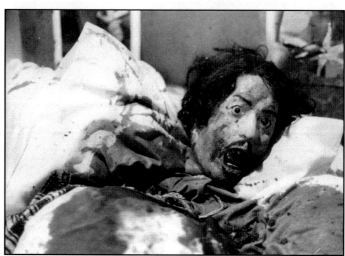

Eyes of a Stranger

In Miami, to film *Eyes of a Stranger*, which was Jennifer Jason Leigh's first major film, Tom got in the best shape of his life. Every morning, he would jog up and down the thirteen floors of the apartment building he was staying in before heading to the set. While on set, he amazed the crew, like usual, by doing unique and realistic effects. The one he is most proud of on the film is a severed head in a fish tank. While using fake heads is necessary in some situations, the viewer can typically tell it's fake in a matter of seconds, which is why Tom always tries to go for real whenever he can.

To make the head in the tank gag look as real as possible, Tom devised a fake shelf unit to hide an actor behind. He then cut a hole in the bottom of a real fish tank and had the actor stick his head through it. The actor had a severed neck appliance glued to his throat to make it look like his head was cut off. Using trash bags and some sealant, he made the tank watertight and then gave the actor a breathing tube. Then, with the help of the crew, they filled the tank up and put real fish inside. When it was time to shoot, the actor held his breath; they removed the tube and rolled the camera. Tom stood just off screen with a hammer in his hand just in case the actor got in trouble, though it was never needed. The finished product looked more than realistic, grossing out audiences around the world.

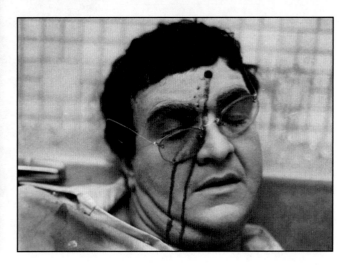

Knightriders was a tale about a group of Renaissance performers who traveled around the country, living life as if they were noble knights, only jousting on motor cycles. Then newcomer Ed Harris played the lead.

Tom recalls the summer they filmed as the most fun he has ever had. He got to ride bikes, joust, act, enjoy groupies, fence with Taso, strap pillows on his ass with Marty Schiff and roller-skate all over the hotel, and just hang out with friends all day long. While the film was poorly received at the time, it went on to get a high viewer rating and find a good following of fans and even a Blu-Ray release over thirty years after its initial run. It would also go down in history as George Romero's *only* non-horror film to date. While the industry finally got to see Tom acting in a meaty role, they still wanted him for what he was best at, his effects. After his summer of fun, Tom was back to killing people that fall.

By Peter Johnson

I still have my armor and it still fits!

While working on *Maniac,* a young concert promoter came up to Tom and asked him to work on a new film. Tom liked the kills in the script as well as the offer, so he shook hands with Harvey Weinstein, who would later go on to be one of Hollywood's biggest producers. The film was about a summer camp... where people got killed. The movie would get labeled as a rip off of *Friday the13th*, but Harvey swore it was written years before. Regardless, the film found a strong following, again thanks to Tom's amazing effects.

The cast of unknown actors included soon-to-be Hollywood stars Fisher Stevens, Jason Alexander, and Holly Hunter. For one scene in particular, Tom had to do Steven's makeup. With Stevens in the makeup chair, Tom played classical music and loved how he found himself speeding up to the music as he did the effects. One of the most famous scenes involved cutting off a set of fingers and killing multiple people on a raft in the middle of a lake. This proved to be tricky, but Tom loved a challenge and made it one of the most memorable scenes in the film.

For the main killer, Cropsy, Tom only had three days to create the makeup and ended up with only two prosthetics to apply, as the oven he used was set too high and destroyed the original mold.

To tell the character's backstory of how he got burned, there was a full fire burn stunt done by Reid Rondell and his father Ronnie Rondell Jr. At this point in his career, Tom had never seen a full body burn so he was thrilled to watch how they did it. They asked Tom to help out by bringing in the torch for them to set the cabin on fire for the stunt. The Rondells had covered every inch of the cabin with rubber cement so it would burn for a safe and convincing effect. Reid was also covered in a safety suit and a healthy layer of the safety fire gel. Tom was simply supposed to bring in the torch and hand it to Ronnie and exit the building.

Getting the signal, Tom ran into the building with the burning torch but slipped on the gel and fell, igniting the entire set on fire. As the flames started to roar around him, Tom watched in awe as Ronnie grabbed his son, held him to the fire, igniting him, then threw him out the door. The man then grabbed Tom and rushed him safely out the back door. Later in the shoot after the Rondells left, they needed a shot of Cropsy's legs burning, so Tom decided to double him. While not a major stunt, Tom still lit his legs on fire for the sake of film.

Sadly, a few years later, Reid was killed in a helicopter crash during the filming of an episode of the television series *AirWolf* at only twenty-two years old.

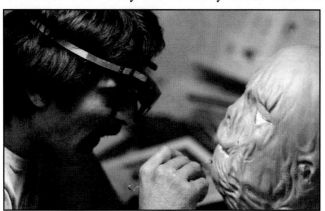

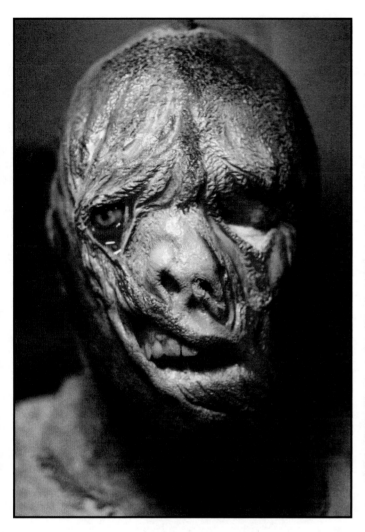

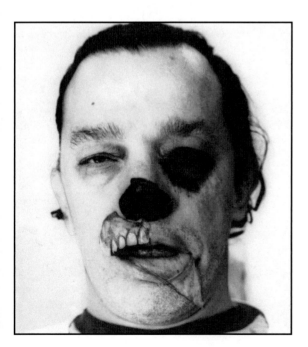

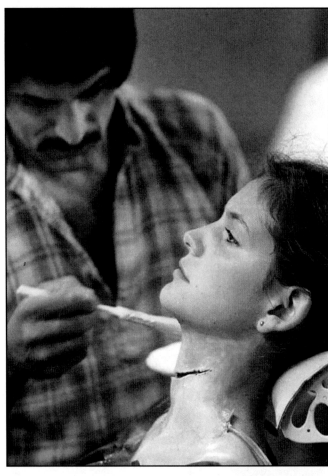

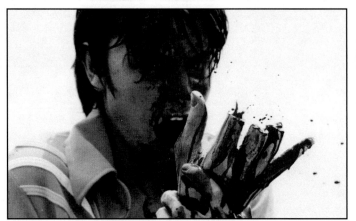

The Prowler

The Prowler contains what Tom thinks is some of his best work. While the plot about a war veteran coming back to kill people at a dance was a bit weak, the film is highly regarded for Tom's ingenious effects. Shot in Cape May, NJ, a place Tom fell in love with and still visits almost yearly, Tom had the task of killing multiple people in various ways, a lot of which were challenging.

One of the most famous effects from the film is where an actress, fully nude, is stabbed with a pitchfork right into her bare stomach. Normally kills involve close ups of clothing that makes it easy for an effect. This gag required Tom to come up with a way to not only have the prongs of a pitch fork go into a bare stomach, but also for blood to pour out. While the answer was actually pretty simple, cutting off two forks of the pitchfork and put-

ting a wooden plug at the end, then running a tube underneath for the blood, the effect amazed and shocked fans. Over thirty years later, the effect still holds up. All these years later, very few effects artists dare to do such a hard effect without the use of CGI.

Farley Granger, the actor playing a role that involved his head being blown off, had to have a head cast done in order to do the effect. At this point in his career, Tom had done many head-casts, though this one would prove to be one of the most difficult. Farley was so claustrophobic that he moved around, panicked, and nearly ruined the cast over and over again. It was the worst head-cast Tom ever did... that is, until he did his next film and had to cast... Stephen King.

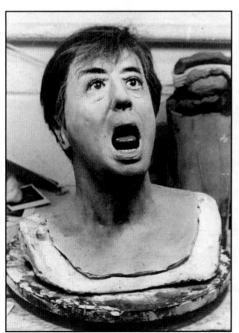
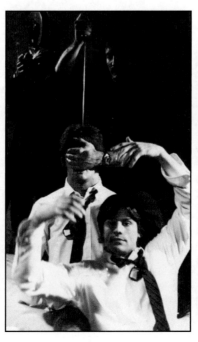
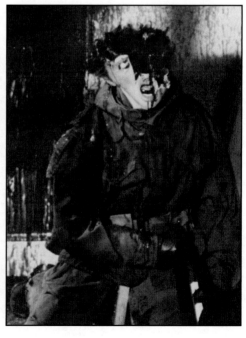

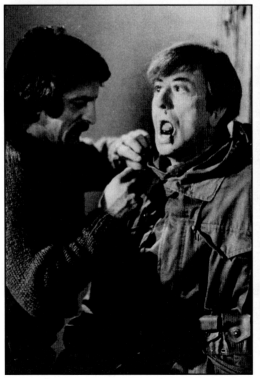 

Creepshow

Once again, George Romero called up Tom to work on a new film, this time with the most famous horror writer in the world, Stephen King. In the early eighties, King was riding high on the success of numerous books and films like *Carrie, Salem's Lot,* and *The Shining*. The teaming of Romero, King, and Savini was a match made in heaven for horror fans. Not only was King going to write the script, he would also star in one of the short films. Tom was sent the script and made his notes on what effects he needed to make, like he normally would do. Only this time, he had an ideal set up: not only was he going to get to shoot in his home city once again, he would have a three month lead in to work on the effects. While he typically had some lead in time, this was longer than normal, allowing him to take his time and experiment with different techniques. It also allowed them to stay ahead of the game while filming, not having to panic and try to get effects done at the last minute.

Set up in an old gym in Murrysville, PA, Tom and his seventeen-year-old assistant, Darryl Ferrucci, were the only two people to work on the effects for the film. Together the two created *all* the effects from scratch, thinking outside the box with techniques like panting peanut shells black to look like cockroaches. For the segment starring E.G. Marshall called *They Are Creeping Up On You*, thousands of cockroaches were required. A team of entomologists went to

105

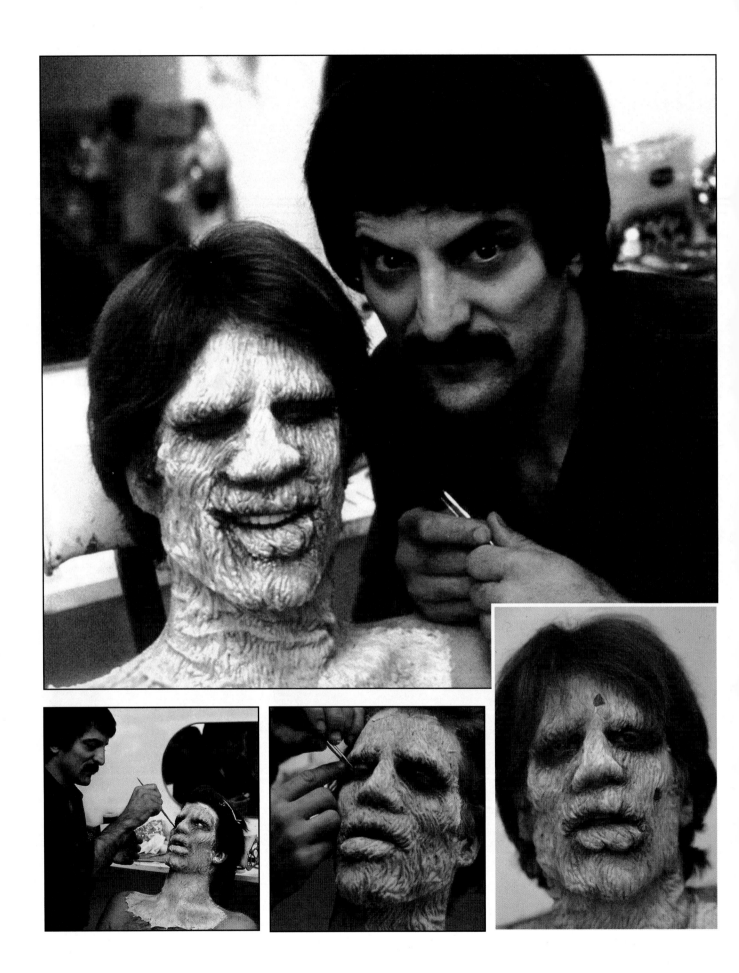

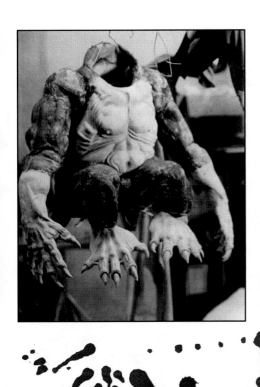

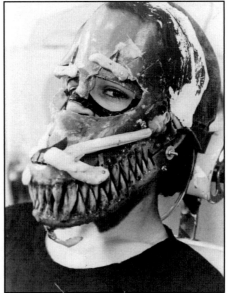

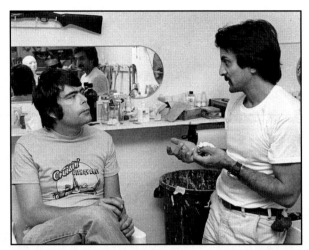

Trinidad and got 18,000 of them by digging holes in bat droppings, shutting off the lights to let the roaches fill the holes, then popping on the lights and scooping them up. Once back in America, they bred another ten thousand more. The crew ended up calling the big bugs "Steves" and the medium ones "Georges," so that way, when they wanted a certain size, George could yell, "bring me a thousand more Steves."

At this point in his career, Tom hadn't really worked with animatronics in his effects. Rob Bottin, who did the effects on the *The Howling*, showed Tom the animatronics he used on the film. Tom eagerly studied his work in order to create one of his all time favorite creations, Fluffy, the creature in the segment *The Crate*. Darryl was inside of the costume moving the head and arms around, while Tom stood off to the side to run the animatronic parts of the character. Fluffy would go on to haunt children's nightmares and become a favorite of fans around the world. To this day, Tom has several sculptures of Fluffy in his house. He even gave one of the original crates to Greg Nicotero, who still has it in his office.

For Stephen's segment, *The Lonesome Death of Jordy Verrill*, Tom had to cast the writer's head. This would prove to be his most difficult head cast *ever*. Stephen could not take the claustrophobia and eventually ripped the cast off his head.

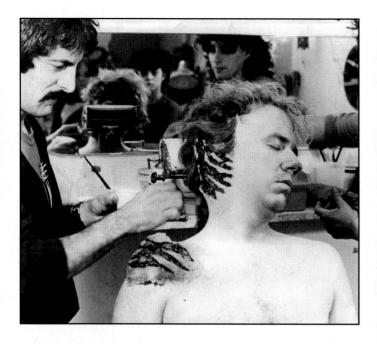

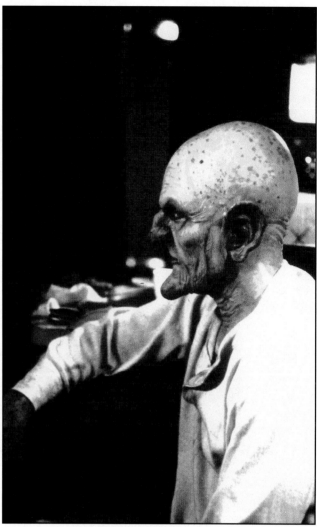

Savini in makeup as The Creep for *Creepshow II*

When it came time for *Creepshow 2*, Tom wanted to do the effects and even campaigned to get the job. Yet for some reason, he was not hired; instead, he was offered the role of "The Creep" and given a "consulting" credit on the film. While Tom loved playing the character, it was a short shoot for him. When it came to the effects, he gave some advice, but the only actual effects he touched were the squibs on the hitchhiker in the segment *The Hitchhiker*.

This is a very rare photo of what was left of Adrienne Barbeau after Fluffy got to her.

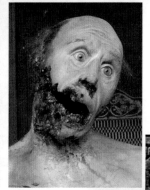

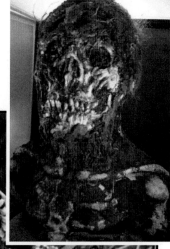

After filming *Creepshow*, Tom got a call from a guy he met in New York. He was going to make a bid to do the effects on a movie in Hong Kong. He asked Tom to go with him. Always up for an adventure and a trip, Tom went for the long flight and took the meeting. They spent a week there, Tom making the producers laugh with magic tricks and jokes. They had seen some of Tom's movies and knew of his work. After going back home, he got a call from the producers: they wanted to hire *him* for the job and not the guy who brought him over there. Feeling badly but not able to refuse an offer to film in Hong Kong, Tom took the job. A few weeks later, he packed up his supplies and took Darryl with him to China.

On the film Tom used a lot of left over props and effects from *Creepshow*. The film, which was titled *Xiao Sheng Pa Pa,* or in English, *Till Death Do We Scare*, was a comedy. Even though it was meant to be humorous, it had dozens of gory and unique effects like a face that implodes, cheeks that get stretched, a hand that swells, and eyes that burst out of a head with flames. While Tom executed his

Young Jackie Chan

job expertly as always, he did have some difficulty with getting items he needed with the language barrier. One day he sent out his interpreter to get some super glue and he came back with...condoms. While he couldn't help but laugh, it was still frustrating.

At first, being in a new country was thrilling and exciting and there were a ton of effects to be done in the film to keep him occupied, but the foreign culture quickly wore on Tom. It was an understatement to say he was more than eager to get home. It was the food. Fish with heads, shrimps with eyes, fatty pig, and other localfoodwasgettingtohim after a while. Halfway through the shoot all he wanted was a damn cheeseburger.

Lunch and dinner ended up being Dim Sum every day: it was horrendous. At one point he even paid an Indian guy he met to cook him some pakora just to have something different to eat. After weeks of this torture, Tom decided to take a left on his walk to the set, instead of the right he always took. A block into his walk, he almost fell to his knees and cried... as there before him was a McDonalds and many other Americanized restaurants. Sadly, it was too little, too late, as filming was done a day later.

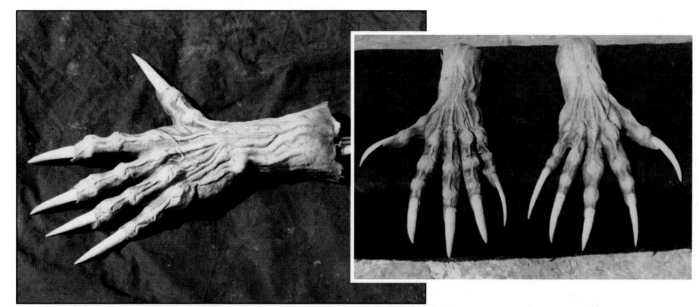

Around the same time, Tom got a call to come back to the series that put him on the map... *Friday the 13ᵗʰ*. By this time, there had already been two sequels to the film. With the idea of being able to kill the monster he felt responsible for creating, Tom took the job and headed out to California and the set of *Friday the 13ᵗʰ: The Final Chapter*.

There wasn't much lead-in time, however, as they had originally hired another makeup artist to do the effects on the film, but the guy disappeared one day when he got the opportunity to do the makeup for a rock star's new album cover. By the time Tom was called in, a very talented crew was already set in place. They were so talented that most of the team eventually went on to start their own effect shops. When he arrived on set, the makeup for Jason was already done and Tom was very happy with how it looked. However, if he said it was done, the guy working on it would be done with his job and have to leave the crew, so Tom gave him another two weeks to "tweak" the makeup.

While Tom had been working in film for years at this point, it was one of the first times he was working on an actual Hollywood sound stage. For him, it was great being on the old Zoetrope studio lot, walking around and seeing other productions working away. Van Halen was rehearsing next door at the time. It was Hollywood, and Tom was loving it. Even Jason was being played by an old industry player, Ted White, who was a stunt man and doubled for greats like John Wayne

and Charlton Heston. While Tom and Ted got off to a rough start, the two became fast friends. Though Ted hated wearing the long fingernails and makeup, he especially hated the fake teeth he had to wear as they started to pull out his aging *real* teeth; regardless, he was a trouper and someone Tom went on to respect tremendously.

Everyone on set *really* thought this was the final *Friday* movie and that they were going to kill Jason once and for all. Of course, the film went on to make so much money, Jason came back the *very* next year... and many more times after that.

A few tidbits from the original *Friday the 13th:*

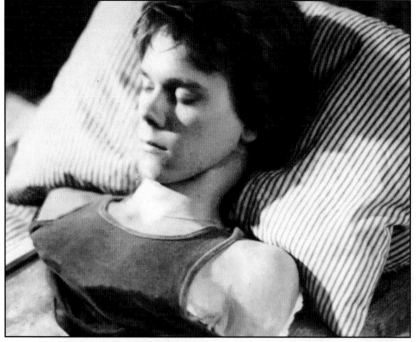

Kevin Bacon before Tom drove the arrow through his neck from behind.

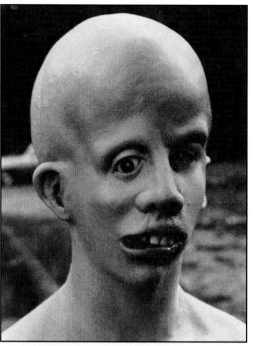

Ari Lehman wearing the final makeup Tom designed for Jason.

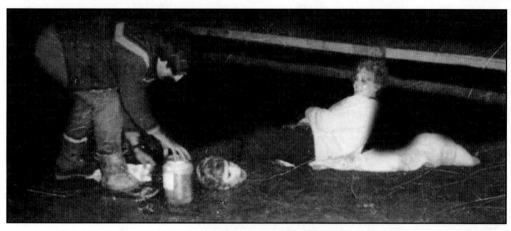

Betsy Palmer, already beheaded and just relaxing after the fight with Adrienne.

Tom prepping to do the stunt for Laurie Bartram where she is thrown through the window.

After *Friday the 13th*, Tom ventured into non-horror, doing effects for a film called *Maria's Lovers*. The film stared Keith Carradine, John Savage, Nastassja Kinski, and Robert Mitchum. Tom was thrilled to work with Robert, but the film wasn't the best experience, as the director was a tyrant and horrible to work with. Some of the effects involved John Savage putting his hand on a stove and a nose bleed for Robert Mitchum.

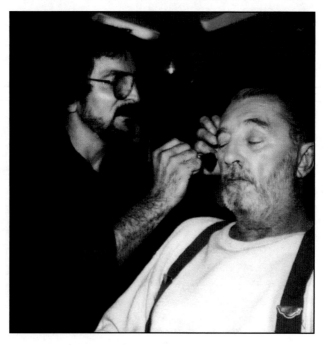
Prepping Robert Mitchum to get a bloody nose.

Tom spent hours running a tube up and around Robert's nose and over his ear to run the blood (all while listening to Robert telling amazing stories about Marilyn Monroe). This delicate work included a fake nose and a wafer thin appliance to cover the tube. Tom did this on the left side of his face, meaning they needed to shoot from the right side. While the director didn't request a certain side, when they showed up on set, he threw a fit, wanting to shoot from the other side. Tom had to re-do the entire appliance. Once it was in place though, they did a take, John threw a fake punch and Robert bled: it worked perfectly. On the second take, however, the tube clogged, and when Tom pushed the blood out, it exploded all over Robert's face, ruining the shot.

A dream sequence required rats. Tom made some rubber rats, but he needed some real ones for the shots as well. He ordered a few rodents from the University of Pittsburgh, but when they showed up, they were white. Tom decided to paint them black by using food coloring so he wouldn't harm them. He also learned how to anesthetize them so he could paint ugly circles around their eyes. The night before the shoot, he painstakingly painted them: they looked perfect. The next day, when he grabbed them to leave for set, they were stark white again. They had licked all of the food coloring off of themselves overnight. Tom had to rush and re-anesthetize them and repaint them. After the shoot, the cute little guys went on to live happy lives on a rat farm (seriously).

A day before the shoot, Tom's doorbell rang. He answered it to find a nice young lady with a clipboard doing a survey. She was from environmental services department asking if Tom or any residents have seen any rodents in or around their house lately. Tom could not believe the coincidence, but the woman was for real. He told her to hold on a second and walked back to his workshop where he grabbed three fake rats. Holding them by the tails, Tom walked to the door and said, "You talking about something like these?" The young girl simply vanished. Tom looked out the door and she was nowhere in sight.

For a scene where John had to have a rat in his mouth, Tom created half a rat with a T bar inside that would fit in John's mouth. By using his tongue on the bar, John could move the rat's tale around, making it look like it was alive. A small toy motorcar motor made the legs kick wildly. When Tom was preparing the effect on set, he wore surgical gloves. The infamous director asked him, "What the fuck are you doing?" Tom said he was about to put his hands in John's mouth so he wanted to be sanitary. The director walked away in a huff, but when he saw the effect, he actually gave a half compliment: "Great, now I can have a dream

After his brief stint in Hollywood, it was time once again to team up with George Romero to make the dead walk once more in *Day of The Dead*. Tom and his crew shot in an underground mine called Wampum Mines. It was a huge storage area underground and just to give you a feeling for the size of this thing, there was a 27-acre lake down there, a big black, pitch black lake. There was also a huge area full of parked cars and huge trucks and there was a storage area for film negatives, Movie negatives, because the temperature down there was always 55 degrees. Tom and his crew set up the equipment in a big room near the offices, and this was after a month or two of Tom and his crew working in Tom's house making generic zombie appliances to use on the hundreds of zombies that would later show up for the picture.

The filming took place in the cavernous spaces where the sets were built. Tom and his crew would not see the sun for maybe two months. It was winter and going into the mines early in the morning and leaving late at night....well, you know, there was no sun. Mine fever affected everyone. Tom would steal one of the golf carts and go after Taso while he was taking a little walk. Tom would come right at him, forcing Taso to grab the cart and flip up over it, walking on the ceiling to save himself. One day in the hotel, Tom and Taso were in the Jacuzzi and devised a plan. They discovered that the jets in the Jacuzzi blew in just air... not water. So, they waited for an unsuspecting hotel guest or guests to enter and they started a conversation with each other about how long they can hold their breath. Taso would say ten minutes, and Tom would say bullshit, and Taso would go underwater and breathe off the jets long enough to panic the guests.

It's a famous story, but in case you haven't heard it, Tom kept a five gallon drum of pig intestines in the studio refrigerator to use in the dream sequence and reality sequence of the autopsied zombie rising up and literally spilling his gut on the floor. Later, they would be used when Joe Pilato, playing Captain Rhodes, would be torn in half. There were some scenes in the picture, like the helicopter landing and the main characters riding down a huge missile elevator to get into the compound. The cast and some of the crew had to shoot those outdoor sequences in Sanibel, Florida, and so, they all traveled there for around

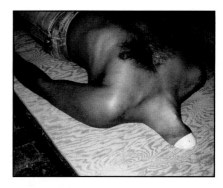

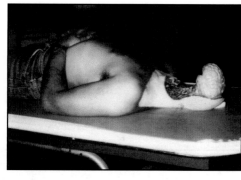

two and half weeks. Once that was completed, they headed back to Pittsburgh and the mines.

When it came time to shoot Joe Pilato getting torn in half, Tom set up the effect by having Joe Pilato's body under the floor and only his head and shoulders and arms exposed on top. A fake body, attached to Joe, was to be filled with the pig intestines. When it came time to put them in the body, it was discovered that someone had unplugged the refrigerator with pig intestines while everyone was in Florida. The intestines had rotted and the smell was justsomething horrible BUT THEY

HAD TO USE THEM.

Where are you going to get new pig intestines and two o'clock in the morning? Tom and his crew wore protective masks to block out the stench, and the zombies killing Joe had wax up their noses and use other such protection. But poor Joe had to go through it without any protection as the viewer would see something like that up his nose. By the time they tore him in half and he spilled his guts, Joe was ready to puke... luckily, he did not.

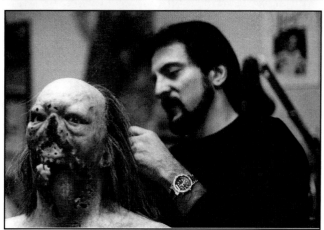

118

Invasion USA and Be Kruel to Your Skool

After filming *Day Of The Dead*, Tom continued his 80's roller coaster of films by stepping out of his normal world of horror and into the world of action by doing a Chuck Norris movie called *Invasion USA*. While it might not have been zombies eating people, there were still lots of effects in the film he had to accomplish with Greg Nicotero and Howard Berger at his side. These included mostly bullet hits, a hand stab, coke straw slammed

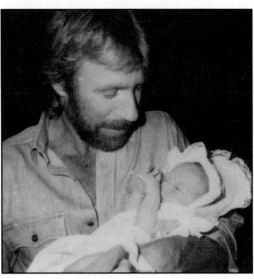

Chuck holding Lia

up a nose, and a guy getting shot through the head. During filming there was this little Mexican actor in a white suit, his costume, who liked hanging around the makeup studio. Tom didn't mind him and even enjoyed showing the guy how they did effects, and this was the guy that Tom had to shoot in the head, or rather, make it look like Richard Lynch was shooting him in the head. Tom did it using an electric match in the gun barrel, a squib on a metal plate in the guy's hair, and a blood bag exit explosion. After that, the guy was done filming his part and left the shoot. The director, Joe Zito, said to Tom, "Do you know who that guy was?" Tom didn't. Joe said, "That was Jaime Sanchez: Angel from *The Wild Bunch*." Tom was flabbergasted: he could have asked him so many questions about one of his favorite movies. Tom enjoyed his time on this big budget action movie and getting to work with Chuck Norris and his brother Aaron. Chuck had great stories about working with Bruce Lee. After the film wrapped, Tom set out to tackle another job he hadn't done before, working on a music video for Twisted Sister and Alice Cooper, The video was for their song "Be Kruel to Your Skool" but was banned from MTV for being too gross. Anytime Alice is in Pittsburgh, he visits Tom's house, as he loves to see all of Tom's toys. How fitting it was that Tom's next project was a sequel to a film that was deemed more than gross...

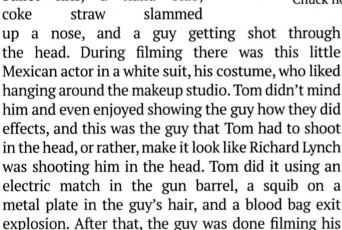

Tom was excited to work with director Tobe Hooper and more than that, to be taking on an iconic horror character like Leatherface.

Tom had a crew member drive an equipment truck cross-country to Texas, where he flew out with his then wife and daughter Lia who was less than a year old at the time. Tom thought Tobe was a trip and loved working with the eccentric man who smoked Montecristo cigars like cigarettes and always had a Dr. Pepper in his hand. In fact, he had a fridge on set full of the cigars and the soda. Tom even gave Tobe a drink hat that could hold two cans of Dr. Pepper with straws that ran down the side of his head into his mouth.

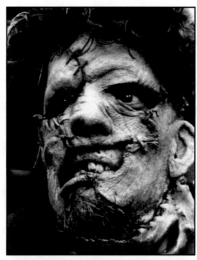

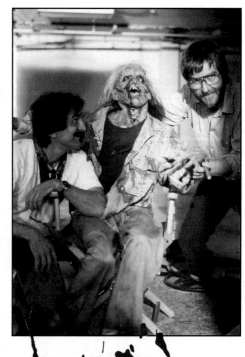

On this film, Tom met his soon to be close friend, Bill Moseley, who agreed to shave his head to play the Chop-Top character, which saved Tom tremendous time doing the makeup. After spending hours in the makeup chair every day, Tom and Bill would go on to play tennis together when they could and stayed in touch for many years. The makeup of Chop-Top, along with Bill's amazing per-

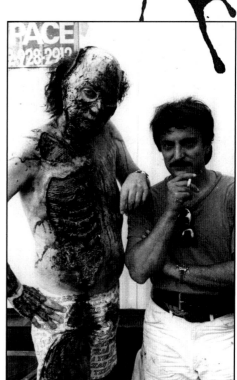

formance, would make the character go on to be a fan-favorite for

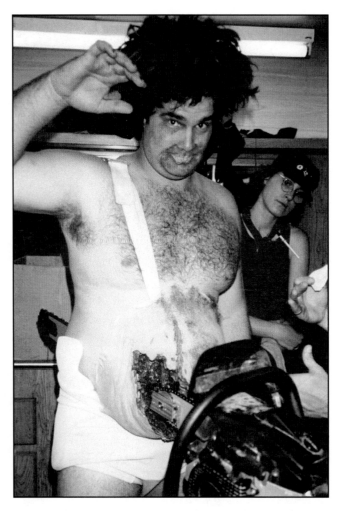

decades to come. It would also cement Bill's career as another horror icon.

For the Grandpa character, the makeup was going to be extensive. Tobe let Tom pick the actor he thought would best fit the character. Tom met and picked Ken Everett, who had long hair and a beard but amazing, sunken eyes that were haunting. The makeup job for the character was one of the hardest Tom had ever done. It took a crew of four seven to nine hours a day to put it on. Tobe said it was the best old age makeup he had ever seen. While Tom didn't sculpt the makeup, he did oversee it and likened the work to the famous 121 year old character makeup on Dustin Hoffman by Dick Smith in *Little Big Man*.

The character that changed the face of horror, Leatherface, was sculpted by Mitch DeVane and overseen by Tom, who wanted a mask that was creepy and realistic, even adding human ears and parts of full faces on the sides of the mask. The mask was amazing, though sadly in the final film, there is nev- er a steady close up of Leatherface where viewers could see all the detail that was there. To this day, Tom proudly showcases the mask on a shelf in his bedroom. He gave the only other screen-used mask to Tobe... for a box of Montecristos.

 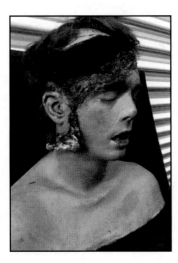 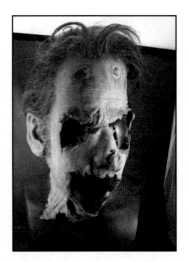 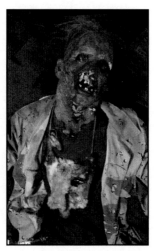

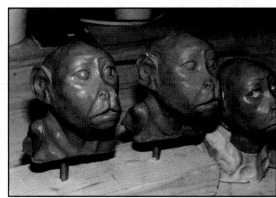

Tom and George Romero once again joined forces to make the film, *Monkey Shines*. Again, Tom had the luxury of getting to work on a major film during the day while getting to sleep in his own bed at night, as the film was shot in Pittsburgh. It was a movie about genetically altered monkeys. They had to use real monkeys for most of the scenes, but the trained ones would only do so much.

The monkeys would do anything and everything for you; as Tom would say, "they would make you dinner, play chess with you, and even do your taxes," but soon as "action" was called, they just sat there. In between takes, two women handlers would walk around with the monkeys on their shoulders. While they were trained to do a ton of stuff, the one thing they didn't have was bowel control. They would just shit any time, anywhere, and to Tom's horror, all over the women holding them.

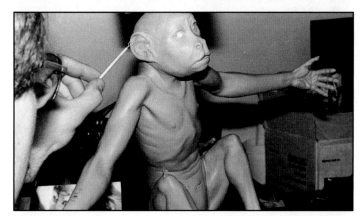

With the monkeys not wanting to act on cue, Tom ended up making a bunch of fake monkeys and arms to use in close up shots; most importantly, he made Robo-chimp, a small, mechanically controlled puppet that George said "saved his ass," since the real monkeys were ruining the shoot. In addition to the robo-monkey and hands, Tom made some fake monkeys he hooked to strings on a stick, like a fishing pole, so he could place one and pull it out of screen to make it look like it jumped or moved quickly. Tom named the fake monkeys Moe, Larry, and Curly; that way, he could just say, "get me Moe for this shot." For one scene he even created an oversized monkey arm

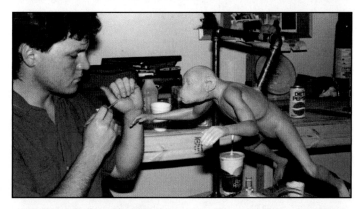

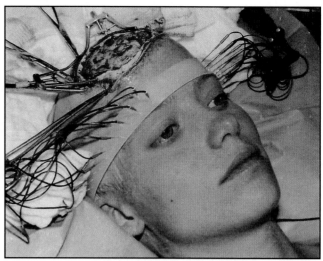

with an oversized razor in its hand, and with the right camera angle, it looked to be normal size. In the final product, you can't really ever tell when a fake monkey is used.

For the ending scene, where a dead monkey was needed to be thrown on the floor, a doll wouldn't do. Tom ordered a dead cat from Carolina Biological (a medical supply company). He gave the cat to the prop people to use in the scene. While it grossed Tom out, it had the proper effect in the final film.

Greg Nicotero was once again Tom's assistant on this film. Greg left medical school to work on effects full-time with Tom. In honor of the life he left behind, George gave Greg a small role as a doctor.

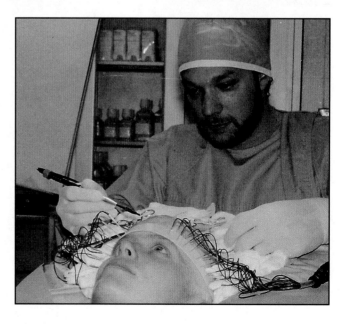

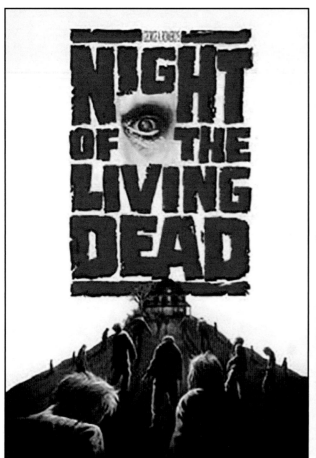

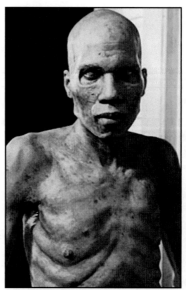

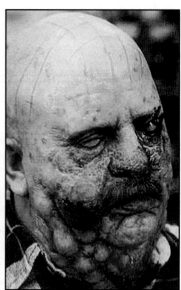

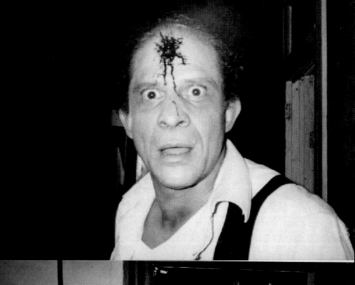

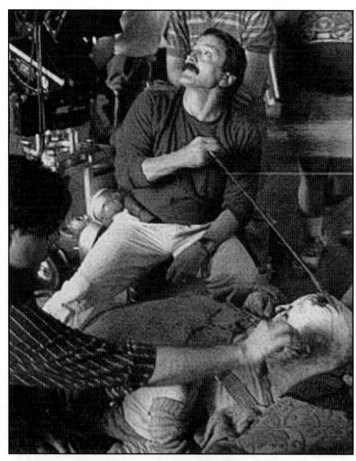

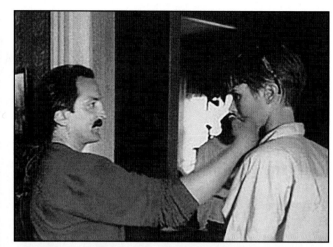

Greg Funk and Piper Laurie

Italian horror legend Dario Argento came calling again. Tom was asked to do the effects on a film called *Trauma*, Dario's second American film after sharing credit with George Romero on *Two Evil Eyes*. Tom had a great

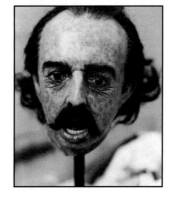

time working with a director he greatly admired, and even more so, was thrilled when he was able shock Dario with his effects.

For one particular scene, actress Piper Laurie's head was to get cut off. A simple trick, though Dario wanted more than just a head coming off. He wanted the head to say "Nicolas" every time it faced up as it rolled across the floor. Tom was set to do a mold of Piper's head, but she was claustrophobic and wasn't able to sit for a head cast. He knew KNB effects had an old cast so Tom borrowed it but really couldn't use it as Piper was much thinner when it was made. Even if Tom could cast the head, he'd have to make it animatronic to make its mouth move. Faced with this dilemma, Tom once again went into magician mode and figured out a solution.

Tom went to the set department and had them build a replica of the floor that he could stand up. Then he took Piper and put an appliance on her neck to look like it was hacked off. From there he wrapped her body in black and painted any exposed skin black as well. He then had her sit on a bar stool that spun and set up the fake floor behind her. When Dario came in, Tom saw the confusion on his face, as Dario was wondering what the hell Tom was doing. Tom had Dario sit behind the monitor and did a test of the shot. Spinning Piper in the seat, he had her say, "Nicolas" each time she faced forward. When Dario saw how it looked, he jumped up and said, "Mama Mia!" From that day on, he called Tom *The Volcano of The Mind*.

126

Tom didn't do any of the makeup effects in this picture but played Sex Machine. This made Tom an international celebrity, and he got work immediately afterward on two other movies in Hollywood. He was now a single parent with a daughter to raise and family always took precedence over those choices.

He reported for duty on *From Dusk Till Dawn*. The first day he showed up at the studio, Quentin Tarantino , Harvey Keitel, and Robert Rodriguez were coming out of the doorway towards Tom and Robert said he had devised this Jackie Chan routine for Tom on a pool table. Without skipping a beat, Tom reached into his backpack and pulled out his cherished photo of him and Jackie Chan from a nightclub in Hong Kong: Jackie was giving the thumbs up to Tom.

HARVEY
KEITEL
GEORGE
CLOONEY
QUENTIN
TARANTINO REGIE:
JULIETTE   ROBERT
LEWIS   RODRIGUEZ
SALMA
HAYEK

FROM DUSK TILL DAWN

Tom was greatly influenced by George Clooney and often says Clooney is the nicest man he's ever met. He saw how little effort it took George to be nice to everyone, and this affected how Tom treats everyone, especially his fans at conventions and other places all over the world.

When Tom turned into the vampire at the end, he had to endure a three-hour makeup job in the hands of his good friend Norman Cabrerra. It was great at the beginning with Tom not minding how much he hates this type of makeup: "it's so sticky" were his outcries. He hates to be sticky from anything: honey, peanut butter, glue. The makeup always felt sticky from the time it went on to the time it came off. In the beginning, he would practice faces in the mirror and run up and down the hallways, sneaking up on people and slowly moving in front of them until they saw this hideous vampire. He even sneaked up on Clooney and then posed with him for photos. BUT... after 16 hours of wearing the foam latex appliances, he was ready to scratch his head off.

Dusk was a tremendous experience for Tom and taught him a great lesson about stage fright.

Having to do scenes with Harvey Keitel or George Clooney could have been nerve-wracking but Tom's attitude was "I can't wait to see what happens... what comes out of me," and that replaced any stage fright that might have happened if he hadn't changed his mindset. Tom often talks about his psychiatrist friend who says all he does all day is get people to change their mindset about stuff. There is tremendous power in that.

One day they were all sitting in the Titty Twister set and Robert DeNiro just casually walked in and sat with Harvey about two feet away. That kind of stuff happened all the time. The KNB effects team drew a heart on the wall of their effects room with a note in it that said "We love Chow Yun Fat", the famous martial arts star. Once day Chow Yun Fat walked in, and of course, they all got their photos taken with him near that heart.

THE JOURNALS OF

TOM SAVINI

GRINDHOUSE

Journal One:

My first day here on GRINDHOUSE in Austin, Texas: Flight down was first class on a small jet. Watched *History Of Violence*, and *Into The Blue* on the plane. *History* was an awesome, grisly, ballsy, sexy, powerful movie. I can't wait to see it again. Picked up at the airport by Cecil, one of the drivers on the show. Brought to the Omni hotel and a rent-a-car was waiting for me here. Room was first class, four-star, and because of the movie/music festival going on in town there are not a lot of rooms available. They are moving me into suite when it's over. All the stuntmen are staying 20 miles away and moving here when the festival is over. I'm on the sixteenth floor, and on my balcony at night, the whole city is like a huge jukebox, with music coming from everywhere and the streets are full of people.

Was picked up and taken to the set around 7:30 and got to watch on the monitor as Marlee, the beautiful girl in the red dress at the beginning of *Sin City*, did a scene with Josh Brolin. When it was over, Josh came out and to my surprise, recognized me and came over to shake my hand. I told him I had just watched him earlier in *Into The Blue*. Robert Rodriguez, the director, who directed me in *Dusk Till Dawn*, came out and we hugged and discussed my look for the film. He originally wanted me to bleach my hair white so I'd look different for this film, but we decided that I wouldn't do that but instead shave off my goatee, keep a Texas handlebar mustache, and get a closely cropped Caesar haircut.

> "It was full of dead bodies, and zombie makeups and severed heads."

We went back to base camp and while waiting for Armand, the head of makeup, to do me, I hung out with Greg Nicotero in the big special makeup effects trailer. It was full of dead bodies, and zombie makeups and severed heads. We hugged and I thanked him for his part in getting me down here and we talked about the possibility of him coming to my school to help Dick Smith in critiquing and helping students in their third semester preparation of final projects. He liked the idea very much. Armand sent word he was ready for me, and I got the best haircut I have ever had, shaved off the goatee, and styled my new handlebar mustache, creating my new look for this movie.

We were driving back to the set to show Robert, and he wanted to see me in my deputy costume, so he sent for Nina, the costume designer, who brought my uniform and right there, outside I took off my clothes and put it on for Robert. I got the thumbs up and joined Greg and his crew for a midnight lunch with the cast and crew. Jeff Dashnaw, the stunt coordinator, came up to me and we talked of all the stunt men we know, and he described how they are going to have this big zombie pick me up and hurtle me 30 feet into the side of a police car. I will have to wear a harness attached to this 70 foot overhead crane with wires and the zombie will pick me up and spin me around in the air and hurtle me toward the car. There will be an automatic stop on the crane, and my stunt double will actually take the hit. More on that later.

Journal Two:

Last night was my first night of shooting, and it was at a police station in a place called Georgetown. I was picked up at the hotel at 5:15 and driven 40 minutes to the location. There were the usual caravan of trailers and huge lighting rigs and cranes, and the station looked like a medieval castle. I was delivered to my own trailer that had a sign outside that read "Deputy Tolo." That's the character I play in *Grindhouse.*

I have basically just stopped eating because the police uniform I wear is so tight. I am eating just salads at the enormous lunch they serve on the set, and this is truly a test of discipline as there is so much food and so many delicious choices, and the desserts... oh my god. But my attitude is, I am doing this movie now, and there will still be food in the world when I am done, and I really want to look as good as I can for this project.

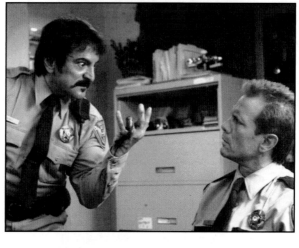

My uniform was waiting for me in the trailer and it is khaki pants with a brown stripe down the side, matching shirt with police decals, and a brown tie and brown cowboy boots. I don't get the gun, pistol belt, and shoulder walkie-talkie until I get to the set. I suddenly realized that I forgot to bring a pair of briefs, and this is not good because as I said, the uniform/costume is tight. I search out the door for Susan, whose job it is to co-ordinate rides to the set, see to our comforts, and provide help to all the actors housed in these trailers. It's me, Michael Biehn (*Alien, The Abyss, Tombstone*), and Michael Parks (*Kill Bill 2, Adam and Eve*, the TV show *Then Came Bronson*). Michael Keaton will arrive sometime to shoot his scenes, then Rose McGowan and Freddie Rodriguez. Quentin Tarantino arrives Monday. I find Susan running around, talking on her walkie-talkie, and explained the problem. Within minutes, Vanessa from the costume department shows up with boxer shorts, and I explained that this is like wearing nothing and I really need briefs and also apologized and said I would not forget my own briefs any more. She returned with a sealed set of black ones and white ones. I thought I'd try the black ones but when I opened the package, one of those big plastic don't-try-to-steal-this-from-the-store security devices was firmly attached to them. I opted for the white ones.

Once dressed I went the special makeup effects trailer where the crew was working on turning a group of stunt men into a diseased sort of zombies, or as Greg Nicotero and I renamed them later, Sickos. They are not really zombies but really disfigured disease victims. I had to have special makeup on my left hand to make it look like a finger was missing.

In the scene tonight, I capture a trouble maker at a local bar who was causing a ruckus, and after I handcuff him, he bites off one of my fingers. Greg, or I should say, Academy Award-winning Greg, personally applied the makeup to my hand and explained that this was the same chopped-off finger appliance they had prepared for Robert Downey Jr. on some previous movie. The top of my finger had to be taped down to the bottom half of my finger and then the appliance was attached and blood added. Todd came in and handed me my per diem (a daily allowance they give you for food and essentials) and after I signed for it and went outside to be delivered to the set for rehearsal, I opened the envelope and I was astounded as to how much they had given me. I'm not allowed to say. Then, Armand, the head makeup artist, suggested that if I left my ear

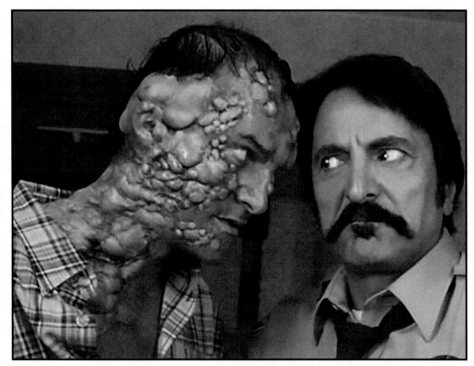
Gino Crognale

Greg, to me the new King of Splatter, came up with the idea of filling plastic soda bottles with blood, and he and his assistant held them in one hand and just punched the bottle and blood splashed/spurted upward. The Sicko/stuntman rehearsed the timing with Greg and his assistant, and I was worried the blood would splash all over me. It had started raining and was cold out, and the idea of getting sticky blood all over me is one of my own personal nightmare. The scene was shot and the stuntman got most of the blood right in his face, and I got just a wee little bit of spatter on my costume: no big deal. We did it over a few times. On the very last take, with a new camera position, the first assistant director called *action* and the stuntman attacked.

Greg and the assistant punched the plastic bottles, and I was drenched in blood. I thank Greg very much for making my nightmare come true: I was standing there, wet from the rain and the blood, sticky and freezing, but it was all worth it when Robert gave me his thumbs up.

Journal Three:

Acting is the toughest job in this business, and as last night proved to me, sometimes the most rewarding. We are still shooting in Georgetown at the medieval castle police station. Georgetown looks like an old western town like Tombstone or something that you would see in an old cowboy movie except with cars. It is easy to imagine maybe around a hundred years ago how you would ride up to one of these old buildings and tie up your horse to some rail and spend some time here.

studs in, I would come across as one of the Village People, so I ran to the set to see if Robert wanted them out. He was seated in the front seat of his new Hummer, and as I approached him, the window came down and he was on his cell phone. I pointed to my ear studs, and he simply gave me the thumbs-down gesture, and I knew they had to go. I ran back to the trailers and Greg skillfully unscrewed them, and I went back to my trailer with my ear studs in a paper cup and waited to be called.

I was driven to the set and rehearsed the scene at the station where I tell fellow officers to go out and get the perp (perpetrator) and book him because "I'll fucking kill him if I have to do it." Meanwhile the perp had broken out of the squad car window and escaped. We approached the car with caution; when my fellow officer Carlos approached the car, we realized the perp was gone and I wanted to know where my finger is. Carlos was attacked by the Sickos and Robert (the director) wanted a spray of blood to splash up into the frame.

"Greg and the assistant punched the plastic bottles, and I was drenched in blood."

135

I arrived at my trailer and got into my costume/police uniform, walked over to the special makeup trailer, and once again, Greg Nicotero applied the appliance to my left hand, making it look like one of my fingers was bitten off. I then visited the regular makeup trailer and Armand's assistant Joe shaved me and applied my basic makeup, touched up my eyebrows and sideburns, and Josh, my stunt double, came over and shook my hand and I didn't recognize him at first. He said, "It's Josh," and I was a little confused at how he looked, and then I realized he was made up to look like me: handlebar mustache and sideburns and dark hair. I said "Are we doing this tonight?" meaning the scene where I am hurtled 30 feet into a police car that implodes on impact. He said, "Yep." I thought it was going to be an interesting night as I would have to do the beginning of the scene where I am picked up by a Sicko, turned upside down, and begin the hurtle toward the car. It was really chilly, and it had started to drizzle and everything was wet.

I got to the set for rehearsal and Tony, the second assistant director, asked me if I wanted a Chai Tea Latte. I was given one the night before and loved it and now it's the first thing I do when I get there. Ah, the perks. The first thing I noticed was a huge crane above the set and Josh attached to a long wire leading down from a traveling rig high in the crane. I was told by the first assistant director, someone I worked with on *Dusk Till Dawn*, to watch how he landed as I would have to simulate his landing in close-up later.

I sat in the doorway of the police station to watch and Josh was hurtled upside down and very fast and hard into the already imploded police car. There

"The most intense scene I had in the movie was not something I was in the mood for right then. But a true professional does the job no matter how he feels, and when the time comes you just gear up and do it."

was a gathering of minds and Josh did it again; this time, after he hit the car, he fell to the ground and hit the top of his head, and this was the only thing he complained about to the medics who rushed over. There was another meeting of minds and Josh did it again with two other stunt guys under the opposite side of the car who held him in place when he hit it with cables they were tugging. Josh did it another few times, and the last time was totally awesome, with Josh hitting with tremendous impact and then falling to the ground onto strategically placed mats hidden in the shadows, and the cast and crew applauded him. They were setting up the next shot where I would mimic Josh's landing when the dark sky opened up with loud claps of thunder, purple lightning, and a deluge of rain. The crew hustled to get everything indoors or under plastic, and I was rushed under an umbrella to a waiting van and taken back to my trailer.

It felt good to be in my nice warm trailer, and I was a little relieved, as the thought of hanging upside down in a harness for the hurtle and then later that night doing the most intense scene I had in the movie was not something I was in the mood for right then. But a true professional does the job not matter how he feels, and when the time comes you just gear up and do it. I got into a comfortable position on my little trailer couch; there was a loud knock and Greg Nicotero came in and said, "Why don't you turn off all these lights?" He proceeded to turn off the lights, and we sat around listening to the rain hitting hard on the trailer and had one of our pleasant conversations about movies and stuff. Greg has been taking really good care of me on this set, making sure when they didn't need me I was comfortable or returned to the trailer. We soon joined his crew for a midnight lunch and I was back in my trailer for a long nap.

I was all settled in and comfy, thinking, well, this is it for me tonight: I will just lie here dozing in and out and they will knock on my door around 5:30 and say it's time to go back to the hotel. It seemed like hours went by and I was alone with my thoughts of that intense scene that I would have to do some day soon but not that night because of the rain. I was worried about the scene because it involved some really intense emotion from me reacting to having just had my finger bitten off and I had to be angry, and the scene was with Michael Biehn and Freddy Rodriguez, and Carlos Gallardo from the original *El Mariachi*. I wanted to do the scene and the fun is seeing what happens when you do something like that, but I was so comfortable lying here and listening to the rain, letting the time pass, that I just drifted off into a deep sleep.

There was a knock on the door and Susan said, "Just want to make sure you were awake because they are going to call for you on the set soon." Shit. I thought she was knocking to tell me they would be

taking me back to the hotel, as surely many hours had gone by. I looked at my watch and it was only 2:30 in the morning. Within a minute or two, I was taken to the set to rehearse. I had to quickly get rid of the cobwebs in my head and wake up for the rehearsal for scene 32, the intense one, the one I was so worried about.

Robert blocked out the scene with us— me, Michael, Freddy, and Carlos— and his energy was inspiring. The video monitors were moved inside a hallway of the police station and it was dubbed the "video village." We would be heading back and forth to the "village" to watch a series of takes Robert would shoot. It didn't take long to get into it, and we did take after take after take. I was screaming, and there were props involved and timed moves to the move of the camera, and the changing of dialogue a bit, and I was screaming more intensely the more takes we did. After about the 30th time, I felt my voice was leaving me and Greg tracked down some throat lozenges for me. We huddled around the video monitors, and

137

Rose McGowan sat there watching the takes and gave me a thumbs up, and that motivated me even more; we did more takes for more coverage when the camera was moved to feature the other actors, and the intensity was building, and the rain was coming down outside, and finally it was over.

This was tough, especially so early in the morning coming out of a deep sleep, but after my gun belt was removed and props took my badge off and Robert was satisfied at the takes, one by one, Freddy, who I'd only known for a day, came over and hugged me and looked me right in the eyes and said "great work." Then Robert announced that I was done for the night and there was applause from everyone. The quiet guys behind monitors and working under tents and people I didn't know because there were so many were applauding, and Robert did his Mexican chant/holler hoopla thing and hugged me and said "awesome." I had no idea it had gone so well because I was just in the scene, so to speak, and just doing it. I was ready to burst into tears. I left the set through a gauntlet of pats on the back. Michael Biehn grabbed my hand and shook his head yes to tell me "good work." I shared a ride back to the hotel in a van with Greg, who sat behind me.

In a quiet moment, Greg just reached over, and in an unspoken show of affection, silently patted me a few times on my shoulder. THAT is what I meant by acting being one of the most rewarding things.

Journal Four:

Tonight was a breeze compared to the night before when we did scene 32, and it might be that the rest of this is downhill for me now. Last night after makeup, I walked over to the special makeup trailer for Greg to apply my severed finger. He came around the corner at me and his face was totally fucked up with large bubbles of diseased growths and pus-filled sores and red and green and yellow discoloration. He was playing a Sicko tonight and said, "We are going to do a quicker version of the severed finger tonight as it is not featured." So, my finger was tied down again with tape and some gel blood was applied and some dripping blood, and I was off to the set, not knowing anything about what we were going to shoot.

As soon as I got there, Brian placed me on top of this big rusty flatbed/tow truck and said that it had to appear like I was just hoisted up there by my fellow officers, and once I was there, I would have to help the other officers onto the truck, and the truck would be moving. Dana, a cute little stunt girl was dressed as an officer, and Josh, my stunt double, was there in uniform and we rehearsed Dana running to the truck and being helped aboard by me and Josh. On the first take, as Dana rushed to the moving truck, I stabbed her in the chest with my right index finger. I was sure it was going to hurt later as I really jammed her hard. On the second take, I stabbed her in the forehead with the same index finger. After "cut," I said, "Boy, I'm really having trouble with this finger."

Robert dictated through Brian that on the next take, on "action," I should stand up on the truck, pull out my revolver, and shoot a bunch of Sickos as the truck is mounted by officers for the big escape. All of us were handed our guns by the gun team, who first showed us the barrels were empty: we are supposed to acknowledge, then carefully close the cylinders and prepare for the scene. On the first take, I helped Dana onto the truck and whipped out my pistol and shot the Sickos, who reacted and fell to the ground. I saw Greg, in all his makeup glory, was part of the Sicko group we were firing at. I said, "Greg, let me shoot you when the truck goes by." He gave me the OK sign. He was wearing a baseball cap, and I told him to put it on loosely and when I fire at him, to jerk his head back so the cap flies off and it looks like I've shot him in the head. He said he was already doing that and told me where he would be coming from, just behind the

> "In a quiet moment, Greg just reached over, and in an unspoken show of affection, silently patted me a few times on my shoulder."

smoldering car. This was the car that exploded the night before. I yelled at him, "I will kill you personally," and it got laughs and became the chant on the set from the crew: *I will kill you personally!*

I told Josh I didn't need to help Dana onto the truck because he was great in grabbing her arm and hoisting her up all by himself. On the next take, Brian yelled *action* and I rose up, whipped out my pistol and firing right at a Sicko near the camera who then whipped past the camera, causing a shadow of a Sicko to pass through the frame. All of the officers and I were firing at Sickos, and when I fired at Greg, his timing was perfect, and his head jerked back and his hat flew off and it felt like I really killed him.

This was better than being a kid and playing cowboys and Indians as we were firing real guns and everyone we shot played dead. We did this scene lots of times and each time, the truck would back up to the starting position, we were handed our guns, and on *action*, killed Sickos.

I went back to my trailer, and after a midnight lunch where I sat with Michael Biehn, who told

Us and Ray Harryhausen

Terminator and *Aliens* stories, I fell asleep there until I opened my eyes and saw my watch said 5:30. I thought this was a short night for me and soon they would be knocking on my door to tell me it is time to go back to the hotel. Almost instantly, there was a knock and it was Susan telling me they wanted me on the set. I was driven the two blocks to the set and saw they were shooting a scene with Carlos on the hood of the police car, but this was a scene before it blows up. He had two or three Sickos on him acting like they were tearing him apart and blood was spraying everywhere. The stuntmen playing Sickos were drenched in blood. Then it was time for my scene.

Robert wanted me to rise up— this is after I have been thrown through the air and hit the police car— whip out my gun, and when I am attacked by the stuntman/Sicko who is drenched in blood, hit him in the stomach with my gun. Bullet squibs would go off on his back, then I would hit him in the chest, another squib would go off on his back, and then I would   uppercut him in the face and he would spit our gobs of blood. We rehearsed the action a few times, and the camera rolled, and we did the take, and it was glorious. I hit him in the stomach and his back erupted with a huge explosion and blood, the same with his chest and another explosion on his back, and then I delivered the uppercut and he spit out the blood and I was drenched in blood once again. It was just like old times.

Journal Five:

Last night was the easiest night on this movie for me, and one of the most exciting. I did not get drenched in blood. Ray Harryhausen, (who, for those of you who have been living in a cave the last thirty years, is the stop motion animation wizard behind such classics as *Clash of the Titans*, most of the *Sinbad* movies, *Jason and the Argonauts*, and many more action fantasy horror movies) is arriving tomorrow and we're all going over to the Alamo Drafthouse theater where he is hosting a showing of the original *King Kong* on the big screen. Everyone is jazzed about this, including Quentin Tarantino who has been here for the last three days. I didn't see him until last night.

I was picked up at the hotel at 7:45 and driven not very far to the armory, right next door to the hangars at the old airport that Robert Rodriguez leases from the state; this is his own private movie studio and where he filmed *Sin City, Spy Kids, Once Upon a Time In Mexico*, and now *Grindhouse*, though so far we have just been on locations around Austin. After makeup and hair, no severed finger appliance tonight, I hung out in my trailer watching a documentary about the Alamo I bought at the Alamo the day before in San Antonio. Around 11 o'clock I hitched a ride to the armory/hospital set to say hello to Quentin. I got there and Joe the caterer hooked me up with his famous chicken potato soup and since I have been starving myself lately, I inhaled it with a quesadilla. I walked into the hospital and the crew and the zombie/sicko extras filled the blood-spattered hallways, and I asked where Quentin was and was told he was operating a camera with Robert on the set. I decided to go back to my trailer, as I didn't want to bother Quentin when he was working like that. It was thrilling to think of Robert and Quentin side by side, operating cameras together.

About twenty minutes later, Susan said they were serving the midnight lunch at 11:30, so I went to the huge circus tent where the crew would eat lunch shortly. I got a salad and sat in the big empty space, and soon the crew poured in. Greg and his effects guys came in, and Greg's arms were spattered with blood and he came to me and hugged me. I checked my costume/uniform for blood. Nothing. I hadn't seen him in a few days and it was always exciting when I did. Soon Quentin came in as I was getting rid of my tray. His attention was elsewhere, so I walked over and squeezed his belly. He turned and saw me and yelled "Tom!" and we hugged. Robert was behind him and said, "After lunch, come over to my office, I want to show you something." I took a seat with the prop guys and showed them I still had the wedding ring on from the other night. They apologized that they hadn't taken it back from me and I said, no way: it was my fault for going home with it.

After lunch, as Robert was leaving, he motioned for me and Carlos to come with him. We got in his Hummer with him and we drove next door to his studio. Michael Biehn, Josh Brolin, and Freddy Rodriguez took a van. As we approached the many gates at the studio, Robert pressed buttons in the Hummer and the gates rolled out of our way. Robert's office is huge, and the big comfortable furniture would not be out of place in a medieval castle. Extra large posters of all his movies decorate the walls along with free-standing, life-size replicas of characters like Marv from *Sin City*; body armor from *Spy Kids* stand in corners, and on one wide brick wall is a huge, impressionistic painting of Salma Hayek. Breathtaking. Robert came in and opened a cabinet under a 80-inch plasma screen TV, pressed a button, and scene 32 came on, fully edited with John Carpenter music added. He used the best takes and we all howled, and then he showed us more scenes he had edited together from other scenes on the shoot. The guy doesn't sleep. When the long shooting day is over, he comes here and edits. An A.D. came in and told us we were due back on the set, and it was back in the Hummer and back to the set. I decided then I must have a Hummer.

> *"It was thrilling to think of Robert and Quentin side by side, operating cameras together."*

We blocked out a scene where Michael, Carlos, and I arrive at the hospital to arrest Freddy, shotguns at the ready. It was a low camera angle shot that Robert would render in slow motion of the hospital doors opening and the three of us ominously walk down the corridor side by side. We did it around twenty five times, and as usual, when about five to ten takes were shot, we huddled around the "video village" and watched the monitors as Robert directed us closer together, or to "move the shotgun to your other shoulder," or to "walk slower."

When he was satisfied, he moved on to another hallway and started using the 30 or 40 extras that Greg and his crew made up to look like diseased, lumpy, moldy, oozing, pus-filled slimy Sickos. I was finished for the night, so I could go back to the hotel. Easy night.

Journal Six:

I love the dreams that happen away from home. You know: the dreams that only happen when you're in a strange bed in a hotel somewhere. Last night, I worked in the studio inside the elaborate set that was built of the interior of JT's Barbecue Shack. Jeff Fahey is JT and he's Michael Biehn's character's brother. All I did was bust into the place as a continuation of when we were actually outside the real Barbecue Shack last month. I burst in, gun raised, behind Michael/the Sheriff who was carrying and aiming a shotgun followed by all the townspeople that we deputized. They were all carrying guns we passed out to them and JT had just killed a couple of Sickos and passed out behind the counter. His dog was lying loyally by his side. After a few surprises, Michael ordered us all to pack up supplies for the hunt for Sickos because we would leave in twenty minutes. That's all we shot and I was there all night.

I got back to the hotel around 6:30 am and passed out immediately and soon, in dreamland, I was on an elaborate Scaramouche or *Romeo and Juliet*-type movie set with everyone in Renais-sance costumes, and I had this elaborate fencing scene where I swung on chandeliers and fenced with this bad guy while trying to win the affection of this lovely brown-eyed arched-eyebrow beauty named Fiorenza. I remember climbing up a wall and hanging onto plants calling, "Fiorenza," but she didn't come out and I was going to be late for my next entrance on camera, so I bounded down this extraordinary staircase. Soon I was skipping down whole tiers of steps and then I was flying high in the air over the stairs and looking for something large and soft to land on, and I looked below and there was Frankenstein's monster, walking on the stairs. What the hell was he doing there? It was my dream so I must have created him there. The dream kind of fell apart after that.

I woke up around noon, went to Gold's to workout, came back to the hotel, and went up to the roof to swim in the stainless steel trough that is the swimming pool. Two lovely dark-haired, bikini-clad deaf girls were lying by the side of the pool, holding hands and... kissing. They seemed very happy. Not only was this the week of the Biker Rally with 40,000 bikers already here, but it was also Gay Pride week with a big Gay and Lesbian parade that day.

The other night on the set, Freddy Rodriguez who has a role in the new *Poseidon* movie, asked me if I had seen it, and I said no. We asked all the extras if they had seen it and no one raised their hands, so I went to see it last night and it was really good and suspenseful; Freddy died much too soon but very well. When I returned to the hotel and fell asleep, this time in dreamland, I was at Disneyworld looking for Greg Nicotero. But this Disneyworld had rides like scooters where I rode magnetic scooters through monumental neon. Then it turned into one of those dreams where you search all night and I never found Greg.

> "...the 30 or 40 extras that Greg and his crew made up to look like diseased, lumpy, moldy, oozing, pus-filled slimy Sickos."

Okay here's what showbiz is (and mind you I am not complaining, as I love every minute of it): sometimes it's just crazy and illogical. I came down here to Texas to resume shooting on *Grindhouse* and I traveled first class and stayed in a suite at a four-star hotel, and they gave me a rental car. I went in for the haircut to shave off the goatee and get down to the mustache to look like Deputy Tolo again. I did the costume and hotel pickup on my second day back and I was on set all night. My action was to run into JT's Barbecue Shack following Michael Biehn/The Sheriff and position myself against a wall, gun-drawn at the ready. I saw the scene on the video monitor and it's good with lots of action and you simply see me in the background backing up the Sheriff.

Then I had a few days off and went to the set last night but they never got to my stuff. Tomorrow I fly home for another break and come back down

here the beginning of July for my final days as the Deputy and my big fight scene leading to my death. I can't tell you how I die, but it is glorious and pretty juicy. Again, I am not complaining, as it was a blast last night to ride the 40 minutes to location: Freddy had Reggae music blasting in the van and I sat next to Jeff Fahey behind Michael. Freddy was in the front seat. We joked that as we approached the location we should crank the music up and rock the van as we pull in. Michael talked about this woman he worked with who was really good and had a scene in the remake of *Texas Chainsaw Massacre* where she blows her brains out, and I told him, "Greg did that" and explained how they used the snorkel camera to pull back through the big hole in her fake head.

Lunch was terrific, and I sat with Robert and Freddy and Rose McGowen and Marlee Shelton and talked about our favorite scary movie things. Rose talked about working in a funeral home and asked Freddy if he did a lot of research for his part in the HBO series *Six Feet Under,* and Michael asked him about an episode where a cadaver had a "hard on." Freddy talked about the special effects penis and mentioned Dirk Diggler's penis from *Boogie Nights* and once again, I was able to say, "Greg did that." Rose talked about this thing she saw where cockroaches come out of this guy and I said, "I did that": she was talking about my special effects work in *Creepshow*. So, I had the opportunity to tell the table about how the entomologist collected the roaches and how we did the effects. Later that night, they blew up a truck which flipped completely over, bursting into flames, and there were about 50 zombie/sickos milling about.

I am having fun and seeing plenty of eye candy and hanging with terrific people, but in terms of how much was shot of my part and what it cost to get me down here for that run into the shack with my gun drawn appearing in the background: figuring the travel, hotel, rent a car, per diem, and my weekly salary...around $20,000.00. You gotta love it.

Journal Seven:

Last night was so much fun on the set. I got picked up at the hotel, delivered, made up and brought right to the set. The first thing that happened was Marlee, who has broken hands, was trying to start her car with her teeth, and as she tried, Jamie, the stunt man doubling Freddy Rodriguez, ran up to her car and yelled, "Help me....help me!" The shot was from inside the car. That was the rehearsal. For the actual take, he was set on fire completely: head to toe— a huge blaze that lit up the night sky. So, over and over again, he was set on fire and ran to her window and sometimes said his line, sometimes he didn't, but the shot was on Marlee inside the car as this guy enveloped in flames approached her and slammed on her window, then stumbled away to the awaiting stunt team that put him out.

The next set up we rehearsed was me and a bunch of stunt guys on that big flatbed/tow truck with all the rusty chains pulling up in front of the hospital. We all jumped off, guns blazing, me with my revolver and some with shotguns, killing sickos while trying to discern which were the escaping patients and which were sickos. The camera featured me confused by all the escaping patients and here and there firing off camera at sickos. At one point, after a car exploded behind me, I turned around fast and shot someone, but it is not a sicko. It was a poor old patient in one of those hospital gowns, wheeling along his I-V stand. I went into a mild shock and then Michael Biehn, playing the sheriff, walked up to me and said "dumbass" and calmly walked away. I did one take as if I've told him a hundred times not to call me that. The crew erupted with laughter.

Before they rolled camera, makeup did touch ups on me, and Greg did a quick severed finger on my left hand and applied some blood, and I climbed onto the truck. Jamie the stunt guy backed up the truck and Tyler, the prop man/gun handler, announced, "The guns are hot" and handed me an electric gun/revolver. These guns were designed to fire a harmless blast of fire from the barrel. You can hold it right up to someone's head and fire and it is harmless. On action, the truck zoomed forward and stopped on its mark and we all jumped off, looking confused as 50 or more extras costumed to look like patients and sickos ran all around us. A car exploded behind the truck and we all reacted to that, and I started random firing at sickos. Another car exploded behind me and on a cue from Brian, the first assistant director, I turned and fired, mistakenly killing the old patient. His chest all bloody, he murmured, "Help me," and collapsed into a bloody heap. The sheriff yelled to all the deputies, "Hey, take control, regroup," and calmly walked up behind me; I am a wreck, and he said, "Dumbass."

So, we did this whole thing again about fifteen times;

sometimes the camera moved to get different angles. It was a calm warm night, and every time they handed me the gun I looked around and saw Robert behind the camera, and Quentin and I marveled at how lucky I was to be there.

Quentin was just enjoying the hell out of all the action and gunfire and exploding cars and dozens of extras running all over the parking lot. It was his birthday and when I went to craft services to get a cup of coffee between takes, I saw the back of this truck filled with all these cakes and candles that Robert's wife Elizabeth made to spring on Quentin at lunchtime. They were special Spanish cakes and Quentin didn't know anything about it.

On around the last take, a car pulled up and Ray Harryhausen got out: THE Ray Harryhausen, as I explained in earlier journals, the stop motion animation wizard behind so many movies Quentin, Robert, Greg, and I and so many others grew up on. We crowded around him and fawned all over him as he cracked many jokes about movies and pulling up and seeing cars explode. We all posed for pictures with him and I could look around and see those in the know explaining to the younger crew members who Ray Harryhausen was.

Lunch was called around midnight again, and I was really eating light because I wanted the cake. Fifteen minutes into it, they brought out the cakes and there must have been a hundred and fifty candles and enough cake to feed the entire cast and crew. There must have been a candle for every crew member. Quentin was floored and we all sang Happy Birthday; he tried to blow out all the candles, and Robert joined in, and every one with a camera, including me, got great shots of the two of them huffing and puffing and blowing all the candles out.

After lunch, Greg cleaned all the blood off my face and unwrapped my finger and I had to put on a clean costume/uniform for the next scene inside the hospital that took place early on in the script, way before the big action scene we just did. It's a scene where the sheriff questions Freddy's character and all I had to do was stand there behind him, holding

"The guns are hot."

a shotgun. Between takes we huddled in the "video village" and watched the scene on the monitors. As they set up the new angles, Robert picked up his guitar, a permanent fixture always alongside the monitors, and played Flamenco guitar for us. We wrapped early and I was back in the hotel. We have the next two days off and tonight I will join a private dinner party with Greg and the cast for Quentin's birthday at Robert's favorite Mexican restaurant, followed by all of us going to a nightclub to hear Robert's sister sing, and then to the Alamo Drafthouse movie theater to see some Grindhouse movies that Quentin is screening. Jesus...pinch me: I am dreaming, as this is all so wonderful.

Journal Eight:

I have to get this out. I've been off for a few days now and lonely as can be... until recently. The days off are so boring compared to being on the set with all that excitement. I believe boredom is a choice, and you don't have to be bored, but not being a drinker and hating the club scene (there are three or four clubs on every block here), I've been watching tv so much that I can recite the repeated commercials.

One of the students from my school, L----, lives down here and when she was at the school, I lusted after her but really couldn't do anything with her because she was a student. Well, she is not a student anymore, and after calling her a few times and having really seductive conversations, we agreed that after one of the night shoots she would meet me at the hotel and "crawl in" with me in the morning. I left her name at the front desk so she could come up to the private floor and my suite. So, I looked forward to coming back in the morning and finding her in my bed, and fulfilling all the fantasies I conjured up all night. I came home and she was not there and not answering her phone. The next night, the same thing; we talked finally and she said I was right that if she went home for a nap first she would sleep all day and I wouldn't

"Jesus...pinch me: I am dreaming, as this is all so wonderful."

see her. That's what had happened, so we agreed that she would make up for it and be in my bed the next morning.

After fantasizing again all night with more delicious things I thought of doing to her, I came back to the hotel, and she wasn't there. Again she wasn't answering her phone. Later in the day I got a text message from her that she was so pissed off that her period had started and she believes in safe sex and coming over was not a good idea. So, I wrote back that I was not waiting for her anymore, and I am flying someone in to be with me. I booked a flight for K---- who would arrive Friday around noon. Later in the week, Thursday, I was driving to Whole Foods and called L---- just to talk and not text to her. She said she was very busy that week but was off that night, so I tried again and asked if she wanted to come over. She said, "If you allow me." She had taken my "I'm not waiting for you anymore" as me saying I never want to see you again. Wrong. Believe it or not, she did come over.

Heaven must be like what happened on Thursday, if Heaven is where your desires and unabashed wishes come true. She brought a bag of lingerie with her, and I really don't care about lingerie and think it's a waste of time and money. After talking and smoking and drinking the wine that she insisted on making me drink, she went into the bathroom and said she would be right out after she changes her clothes. I was sitting on the couch facing the doorway to the bedroom and to the left of the door was the bathroom. I waited and waited, my eyes fixed on the doorway, my camera in my hand, and I was excited when I heard the door open and the light go off in the bathroom. The vision that came around the corner and posed in the doorway caused my involuntary reflexes to contort me into a sitting fetal position and I groaned at the pleasure that filled my eyes. I forced composure on myself and took a series of clumsy photos that will never do the real thing justice.

She paraded around in these high heels that really were the most she was wearing, and I couldn't take my eyes off of her. We drank some more wine, and

Jeff Fahey, Josh Brolin and Michael Biehn

kissed and teased and kissed and teased and looked out the huge floor-to-ceiling windows that overlooked a huge drop, seventeen floors down into the lobby, and it made her knees weak. I couldn't take it anymore, and the next time she kissed me I moved her onto the floor and laid her down, and for the next hour and a half produced a lot of groans and screaming and wetness and penetration and kissing and probing and sucking and wildness and grabbing, and at some point in there, we moved to the huge window overlooking the lobby seventeen floors down and I pressed her naked body against the window, leaving titty prints on the glass, and back to the bed for more assault with a friendly weapon. Then I calmly, silently, gently played with her hair and moved my hands all over her and we settled on a position with her head on my chest and I continued to slide and glide my hand gently on her back and petted her and we whispered cute nothings, and talked and laughed, and soon started all over again, and again later.

She said she had to work the next day, which was really just a few hours later since it was around six in the morning. She said she would come back later but I had to tell her K---- was coming in, and she didn't like the idea but understood that it was because she didn't show up those last two times.

We made arrangements for a few days from then for the Alamo Drafthouse when Ray Harryhausen was hosting a showing on the big screen of *King Kong*. It turns out it was Quentin's birthday so that night turned into dinner at Robert's favorite Mexican restaurant. L----- wasn't there because it was really an intimate dinner with Quentin, Robert, and the cast, but she hooked up with us later at a club called Antone's where Robert accompanied his sister for a few songs on his guitar, then the Alamo Drafthouse theater where Quentin showed one of his favorite Grindhouse sexploitation movies, *The Girl From Venus* or something. Some of it was funny but I would have enjoyed it more if I didn't want to get L----- back to the hotel. She turned to me and said, "Do you want to go back to the hotel?" The next thing I knew, we were there and Greg came with us and we got on the computer and showed him her stuff on My Space, and when he left, we went back to heaven. This time was even better than before as the wine last time, combined with performance anxiety, affected my/Jason's performance. I named him Jason because just when you think he's dead, he comes back to life.

145

Journal Nine:

Well, another day off and another day looking for something to do. I thought this was going to be a dull evening with me working out, ordering my daily chicken Caesar salad, maybe trying to see a movie, and then letting TV put me to sleep...but then came Courtney, and boy, was I wrong.

I did drive out to the movie theater but it was late, around ten o'clock, and all the features had already started and I was really hungry, so I was torn between going to the Yellow Rose, a classy strip club down here, or back to the hotel for my salad. I chose to go back to the hotel and turns out that was THE right thing to do. The restaurant was closed so I went into the hotel bar and ordered my salad. I could have just said "the usual" and they would have known what I meant as it's been a routine for me there. The waitress brought me my diet Coke and I looked across the room at the bar and saw this petite blonde woman sitting there in a silky dress holding her head up with her hand, her elbow on the bar as if she was depressed or angry or tired. I got up and walked right up beside her to get some lemons from the bartender for my Coke, but I really wanted to see what she looked like. As I approached the bar I stared at her, waiting to get a good look at her face, and as I approached, she turned to look at me and I looked away. What I saw before I looked away was a look-a-like for Jennifer Aniston.

I got my lemons and went back to my table, and almost as soon as I sat down, she got up and walked toward me and said, "I'm sorry, I hate to bother you, but are you Robert Rodriguez?" I laughed out loud and said no, but I am working with him right now on a movie here in town. She said, "No you're that makeup guy: I love your movies" and she got my first name right but couldn't remember my last so I told her, and she said to forgive her but she'd been drinking. I was hoping she would sit down, and almost as if I willed it, she put her hand on the top of the chair opposite me to move it, and I quickly said, "Please... sit down." After the "what movie" and my asking "what are you doing here" stuff, she told me she had just had a fight with her friend. I said, "Male or female?" She said, "Male." I said, "Where is he?" She said, "Taking a shower, but he's not my boyfriend: he's just a friend of mine, and I'm with

him because he's so smart. He a psychology major doing research here mainly in sociology and I came down here with him to show him Sixth Street."

I felt comfortable telling her to forget that guy and come up to my suite and we'd have a little adventure, a mini-vacation. She loved the idea but felt she didn't want to just dump him, so how about "I'll take him to Sixth Street and have a few drinks and then come see you." I said we better quickly pick a time before he shows up. We looked at my watch and it was a little before eleven, so we decided on 1 o'clock. I took back my card that I handed to her and wrote my cell phone number on it.

Her friend came into the bar. He was a rotund man with jet black hair and huge black beard, and she introduced me and showed him my card and he kept it. I said it was alright and gave her another card, and she told her friend she needed the first card back and she would give him the one I just gave her. He said, "Why, is this a special card?" She said yes and quickly took the card back with my phone number.

"I'm sorry, I hate to bother you, but are you Robert Rodriguez?"

He started asking me about horror movies and do I think the latest ones are any good, and do I think humor and horror are a good mix, and my mind went into automatic mode and signaled my mouth to start spewing all the auto-responses to such questions I've practiced so many times at all the horror conventions I've attended. In the meantime, I would look at her occasionally with the secret bond we established before he showed up, and I started rubbing her leg with my hand under the table while answering her friend's questions. She put her hand under the table to stop me, saying under her breath, "hairy." I continued feeling her leg, showing her I didn't mind. Soon after, she told him, "We better go," and before they left, she hugged me goodbye and whispered in my ear, "I'll see ya soon."

She called me from the lobby at a quarter to one and I met her on the twelfth floor to escort her up to 17, the private floor and my suite. Before we entered, I stuck the key/card into the slot and told her, "You

146

know what, when we get in there, there's going to be sexual tension, so kiss me right now and get it out of the way." She thought this was funny and kissed me passionately and long and went into my suite. That's a good line and I learned it from watching Woody Allen's *Annie Hall*. It works. As soon as we got in, I continued kissing her and feeling as much of her as I could standing up, and I strolled her into the bedroom and we laid on the bed kissing and touching. I explored her silk dress, manipulated her panties off, and started kissing her nether regions and she said she didn't like that, and ever so politely, I wish I could remember her words, told me she really likes my work and likes me but that she needed a cigarette and a drink and would like to relax a bit and talk, and that I could kick her out whenever I want and she is sorry if she was disappointing me. I realized I was moving too fast and assured her I know what "no" means, and I wanted her to trust me and more importantly, feel comfortable with me.

> "Quentin brings in some of his 35mm film collection and shows them at the Alamo Drafthouse."

We sat on the couch and I kept my distance and told her she could help herself to the minibar, and we smoked and talked and laughed and I stared her right in the eyes and listened to everything she had to say as if it was the most important thing going on. She asked me about me as she thought she was talking too much about herself, and the conversation glided into her already telling me what she doesn't like and that maybe she should tell me what she does like. And that was the beginning of the dream coming true. We went back into the bedroom and that silky dress became a chair decoration, and she let her hair down, and so went my pants and shirt and her 23 year-old toned and tanned body circumnavigated every inch of my huge pillowy bed. Earlier she said she liked a manly man who takes control so I skipped that particular audition and just did it, and she really knew what she wanted and liked it gratefully.

We left a wake up call for ten a.m., and around eight a.m., we still hadn't slept we were so wound up. The night was filled with trying to sleep but every time our legs touched or we rolled closer to each other something made us start kissing or fondling and that always led to much wetness and more sex until we got tired and tried to sleep again. I ran out of condoms at one point but luckily found three more in a suitcase compartment, and it wasn't long until they too decorated the floor along with empty Fiji water bottles.

Exhausted, she said she should probably go back to her room so she could get a little sleep and see what the day was going to be like. She had to meet her father and get her birth certificate so she could get a passport as she and her friend might be going to Europe. She got dressed and left me her phone number so I could come to her section of Austin and stay at her place Monday night after she got off from work. She worked at a piercing/tattoo place and danced at a club one night a week and that would be Monday. We kissed goodbye and said how nice it was to meet and she left around 8:30. I fell into a deep sleep until the phone rang at ten with the wake up call, and then fell again into dreamland until four in the afternoon when I woke up and just lay there, rethinking the night before, smiling.

Journal Ten:

I've been off for a week and went back to work this past weekend. Our work week is Thursday to Monday and that is a five day week, and we are off on Tuesday and Wednesday and that's our Saturday and Sunday.

On Tuesday nights at midnight, Quentin brings in some of his 35mm film collection and shows them at the Alamo Drafthouse movie theater here in Austin. He does that so the crew has something to do and really something to keep them awake on our nighttime shooting schedule's days off. Last week, he showed his print of *Carrie* and then I think *Revenge of the Cheerleaders* or something like that. I didn't stay for that one.

My days off have been filled with interesting things happening. My typical day is I get up, I check email and write a journal entry from the night before, go to the gym and do cardio on the treadmill or the sitting bike, and then workout a body part, like Monday is chest, Tuesday is arms and so forth.

The gym only has dumbbells and a bench and the aerobic stuff, but even so, I've lost sixteen pounds in the 25 days I've been here because if you remember from the day I tried on my costume/police uniform, I decided to lose weight and now that uniform is loose and that's exactly what I wanted to happen. Then, I return to my suite and I either order a grilled chicken Caesar salad with iced tea, or I drive to Whole Foods and get a spicy white chicken noodle bowl, and that's it until I am on set and eat more salad.

There's been Quentin's birthday where we all went first to this Mexican Restaurant and Quentin got his first pair of cowboy boots, and I sat with Jeff Fahey and Greg Nicotero. Robert had a Mariachi band come over and serenade Quentin and they sang "Happy Birthday" in Spanish. We had a little celebration the night before on set at lunch with those hundred or so birthday candles, but that night it was a very long table with gobs and gobs of Mexican food that I faithfully ignored until Greg offered me some of his beef enchilada and I succumbed to the smell and helped him finish his plate. Then it was on to Antones, a nightclub where Robert's sister was performing and from the VIP room above the club, we watched her with Robert accompanying on an electric guitar. We hung out there with the cast until around midnight and then went to the Alamo Drafthouse for Quentin's showing of a sexploitation flick called something like *The Girl From Venus*. I only made it halfway through that and walked back to my hotel and crashed.

Then there was Robert's Art Exhibit which benefited a charity I can't recall right now. We were picked up in vans and taken to San Antonio to one of Robert's favorite Mexican Restaurants when he was growing up and this was not the elegant Mexican place from the other night but a little mom and pop place that was tiny and sparsely decorated with tables arranged in a long room. It seemed like Robert just rented the place for the night as we were the only customers. I rode down with Michael Parks and his wife and it was like I was riding with Sheriff Muldoon from *Kill Bill* and *Dusk Till Dawn* as Michael has a charming, down to earth conversational tone. I pigged out at this restaurant and then we were put in individual SUV's and driven to the red carpet outside the art gallery with tons of photographers and reporters, but beforehand, we were instructed not to talk about the movie. It seemed strange to us to be there for the press and not to talk about the movie, but we did it and I'm sure it's to help the secrecy thing about this film.

"Robert's paintings, around twelve of them, were the same pose of Salma Hayek but rendered differently, and were stupefying, amazing, phantasmagorical, twelve feet-high, jaw-droppingly gorgeous."

Robert's paintings, around twelve of them, were the same pose of Salma Hayek but rendered differently, and were stupefying, amazing, phantasmagorical, twelve feet-high, jaw-droppingly gorgeous.

This man never stops amazing me. There is more talent in one square inch of him than most people have in a lifetime. I saw someone photograph one of the paintings and realized we were allowed to and shot all of them. Later, after emailing my daughter Lia some shots, she fell in love with one of Salma as the Sacred Heart. I emailed the gallery director for a price and it was somewhere in the neighborhood of $25,000. Let's see... new Hummer or painting for Lia?

Reporters took lots of photos of me and Michael Biehn and Josh Brolin and Jeff Fahey together and we decided we weren't going to stay for a private reception and went back to Austin. I rode with Josh Brolin and had a fun conversation with him for the hour trip back. He left for L.A. the next day and within a few more days I was back on the set. I got into my costume/uniform and into makeup, and had my severed finger applied but they didn't use me at all. This was starting to worry me because I was anxious to get home for Lia's birthday on the 11th. This was Saturday the 8th and there was a big scene to shoot; this was to be my last night on the set and they didn't use me. Brian asked if I was available the next day and I cheerily replied, "Of course darling," but I was worried.

The next night, the same thing occurred with costume and makeup, but this time, I was immediately taken to the set for the rehearsal of a complicated scene. The big flatbed rusty tow truck turns a corner and comes down a hill to me and Michael and a dozen townsfolk while I carry a shoebox full of badges and two duffel bags of guns into the scene and ask Michael, the Sheriff, if he's sure he wants to do this, and he says yes and we deputize the townsfolk and pass out the guns, except to Freddy, to whom Michael says, "Except you Ray." Michael turns his back and Rose McGowan, playing Dakota, slips him one of the guns and I quickly snatch it out from behind his back where he hides it and say "Nope," and we all proceed up the hill, guns in hand, to JT's Barbecue Shack to fight and kill the sickos who are hiding there. At one point I joked to Robert that the bag of guns didn't contain the Dick Gun I wore in *Dusk Till Dawn*. He seriously considered putting it in and asked if I had mine with me. I said no, and he said his was at home, but maybe when we get inside the barbecue place I could find it and do a take and toss it aside.

This scene took most of the night because the truck's brakes gave out twice and then the back up truck was brought in and its brakes gave out as well as its power steering. So the scene is the truck coming down the hill; Robert, behind the camera on a dolly on tracks, backs up in front of me and when the truck passes, I cross the tracks to Michael and say, "You sure you want to do this?" He says, "Break 'em out" and I take the box of badges and slam it onto a pick-up truck. I throw the duffel bags of guns on the truck and another deputy distributes the guns and badges to the townsfolk. We did maybe twenty takes and then the camera was moved on top of the hill so that before lunch we did take after take of all of us running up the hill. It was a good workout.

As we move up the hill, Michael/the Sherrif says something like, "Be careful, don't shoot yourselves, and especially...don't shoot me."

I do a take and mouth the words "dumbass" and slipped and fell. Robert and Quentin thought that was funny for some reason and insisted I leave it in. So here I am, trying to look cool as the deputy running up the hill with my gun at the ready, and I have to trip and fall on my face every time. We did this endlessly and then we had a break while they shot the barbecue hut engulfed in flames as Rose escapes past the camera. Some sickos are shot and the camera finds her again, but only this time it is her stunt double Dana, and Dana runs down the hill and falls and rolls head over heels. Rose is wearing the skimpiest leather mini-skirt and a small top and it is freezing and there is a reason women like her are famous. She is really, really hot and gorgeous and beautiful and friendly. Dana, in her stunt double costume of Rose, is not so bad either and very nice to look at. I spent some of my lunch hour tracking down Rose to get a shot of us together, and she emerged from the makeup trailer and was happy to let Susan photograph us but warned, "Don't get any blood on me." I happily obliged.

After lunch, I sat at the video village on top of the hill with Jeff Fahey for a while and watched the sickos Greg and his crew prepared do their shtick. Jeff was talking about his favorite colors of jelly beans and I asked the set

"Be careful, don't shoot yourselves, and especially... don't shoot me."

149

coordinator Tony if he could get some jelly beans for Jeff. It was getting really cold and I went to the craft service truck to get some hot soup, check on Jeff's jelly beans, and then to my trailer to put on some thermal silks when Susan knocked on the door and said I was wrapped and could go back to the hotel. Me and Jeff, who was handed jelly beans in the van, and Michael and Freddy and a bunch of others were driven back to the hotel. I packed and was on a plane that afternoon and got home just in time to watch James, my grandson, so that Lia could be taken to dinner and out that night with co-workers for her birthday. It is now the day after her birthday and I still haven't seen her. Tonight I will take her for a birthday dinner and then home to the cake I had made for her with one of those food coloring photos on top of a montage of twenty photos of her from a baby to the 21 year-old woman she is today.

In about a week or two, I will travel back to Austin for pickups and my death scene that takes place inside the barbeque hut.

Journal Eleven:

Well, I'm back in the saddle again. (Sung to the tune of "Back in the Saddle Again"): Everybody sing. *I'm back in the saddle again...Oh I'm back in the saddle again.* Okay...stop...stop singing. I am back in Texas again to continue shooting *Grindhouse.* I've had plenty of time during the last hiatus to grow the goatee back and the hair on my head, and I've lost 25 pounds and my abs have happily returned, and I, and everybody else, am happy to be back.

Saw Michael Biehn in the elevator and then in the lobby and he is staying here now. The deal is, for me and for him, it's either a suite here at the Omni or a room at the Four Seasons. We happily chose a suite here and we both joined Gold's Gym about two blocks away. The hotel gyms are not that great. Went to the studio and met Robert in his office and he is doing just great

and chomping at the bit to start up again. Shook hands with lots of folks who are back and who I haven't seen in over a month. I was in the A.D.'s office and someone grabbed me from behind in a bear hug. It was Greg. I went with him to his special makeup trailer, and he and his crew were unloading some of the most grotesque body suits and masks I've ever seen. The world isn't ready for this movie. I stopped in to see the stunt guys and they gave me a taco, and Jeff, the stunt coordinator, showed me on his laptop just how the zombie/stunt man is going to lift me and hurl me into the police car. Josh, my stunt double, had me try on the harness I will wear when they attach me to the wires and crane. Steve Jacobson, the stunt coordinator from *Dusk Till Dawn,* was there and we hugged.

I am trying to hang onto my goatee as long as possible. I think I look like a Mexican turtle without it. I was scheduled to shoot tonight more of the scene at JT's Barbecue Hut where we deputize the townsfolk. I got ready at 4:30 for a 5:30 pickup by shaving off the goatee and showering, and I got a phone call from David, the second A.D. who told me they cancelled the outdoor shoot and are going inside the cover set at the studio, and I am essentially off until Monday. Today is Wednesday. 'Could have kept the goatee longer; hell, could have stayed in Pittsburgh longer.' That's showbiz.

My plan is to spend the time working out, shopping, and going to the studio tonight and hanging out with Greg. He is off tonight as well but it's more fun to be at the studio around Robert and the crew than hanging at the hotel.

Aha! David just called and I AM working tomorrow night. Scene 46 is something that was planned to shoot sometime in July. It's been raining a lot down here and they are looking for stuff to shoot inside the studio as rain cover. I went to the studio, getting lost a few times, and hung out around the video monitors. Joe, the makeup guy, said I looked so young and did I have work done and I told him no it's because I lost some weight. I didn't want to tell him it was 25 pounds. The general consensus was that everyone is glad to be back and working on this project again. Robert came off the set and saw me and did an evil laugh, which I returned. He shook my hand as he walked to the video monitors to check the scene he just shot of Freddy Rodriguez, who enters the barbecue shack, sits next to a dog on a stool, and eats barbecue that Jeff Fahey was feeding him on the counter. The dog kept getting up and blocking Freddy. Greg Nicotero was sitting next to me and said, "Dogs and kids" calling attention to the old film idiom about never working with dogs or kids. I said, "Or monkeys," reminding him that we worked with all those damn monkeys on the movie *Monkey Shines*. Robert sat in front of the monitors, making lighting suggestions and camera moves while playing classical flamenco music on his guitar. It's good to be back in this environment.

Today I woke up late and worked out at Gold's Gym a few blocks away and came back to swim in the hotel pool. It's on the roof of this place and it's essentially a stainless steel trough, and the Jacuzzi is a stainless steel pot. I am sitting in the Jacuzzi with a huge guy with the words "Travis" and "Jesse" tattooed on his back. "Travis" takes up his entire upper back from shoulder to shoulder, and "Jesse" takes up his entire lower back. He asked me if I was a biker as he is and just drove his Harley from Las Vegas.

Today was the beginning of a Harley bike rally here in Austin and they are expecting 60,000 Har-

ley bikers. The hotel indoor lower level parking garage is full of bikes already. So, we are in the Jacuzzi and lightning starts flashing all over downtown Austin. We looked at each other and he said, "it's not safe to be in here, is it?" I said no because we are in water in a huge stainless steel pot. He got out but I stayed in as two lovely young bikini-wearing, dark-haired beauties climbed the ladder to the Jacuzzi. I warned them that lightning was flashing in the sky and getting closer. They indicated to me in sign language that they are deaf. So, here I am, in this stainless steel pot on the roof of the hotel with this big biker, standing just outside a Jacuzzi: it's me and these two lovely ladies in bikinis and I am doing a charade act, motioning to the sky and indicating something horrible with my hands coming out of the sky into the Jacuzzi. They seemed to understand and were oblivious as I watched lightning flash behind them, followed by loud claps of thunder that they did not hear. When I left, which was quite soon, they were happily sipping their drinks and having a happily animated sign language conversation.

Journal Twelve:

Yaeeeeyyy! I am back in Austin, continuing to play my part in the Quentin Tarantino/Robert Rodriguez movie *Grindhouse*. I flew down here with Gino Crognale; I call him Onig and he calls me Mot... that's our names backwards. I don't know why we do that but we always have. He was working on another movie and has now joined Greg and the other KNB guys on this movie. We've been friends ever since I hired him for *Texas Chainsaw Massacre part II*.

Last night I flew, and it wasn't on any airplane or in any dream. I'll explain. Got to the set around 9:30 P.M., rode in the pickup van with Freddy Rodriguez, got some coffee, and went to my trailer. On the counter was a new set of black undergarments I'd never seen before or worn. There was a note from the stunt department: "Tom, please put these on under your costume as we are putting you into a harness tonight." It was a long pair of black, tight, rubber-like underwear and black bicycle shorts. I put everything on and it was immediately hotter for me as the temperature outside was around 101.

"...it's not safe to be in here, is it?"

I hung out with Greg and the effects guys for a while. They had just driven a stake into Quentin's right eye the night before. I was there, as sitting around in the hotel is not as exciting as being on the set, and I came out to the studio last night and the night before.

Later that night, Quentin is about to rape Rose, but he is infected with the zombie juice and his body starts to melt, including his dick, which turns into this long stretched-out, lumpy, squirting thing. Then he pukes out this ghastly, membranous, tentacled blob of multicolored goo. The world is not ready for this movie.

They called me to the set which was out near the runway of the sound stages that Robert owns, and I saw this high crane positioned over a reproduction of the police station exterior that I worked on months ago. I rode with what they call the first unit. That means the lead actors which tonight includes me, Michael Biehn, and Freddy Rodriguez. There was also dozens of extras and stuntmen made up as zombie/sickos. Everyone got final touches from wardrobe and props except me, as I had to drop my drawers as the stuntmen fitted a harness onto me that would be hidden under my costume. Once they were finished and I was dressed again, Vanessa, the on-set wardrobe person, cut holes into my costume at the hips, and the stuntmen attached small D-rings onto the harness underneath. This will be the scene where after Carlos is attacked and his arm is bitten off, in shock, move to try to retrieve my wedding ring from the fingers of Carlos's severed arm and a zombie/sicko grabs me and hurls me thirty feet into an imploding police car. Josh, my stunt double, already did the upside hit into the police car months ago; now we have to shoot the beginning when I am grabbed and lifted into the air and tossed. Josh does it first so we can see what's going to happen, and it was pretty smooth as he was lifted and spotted by other stuntmen circling the stunt pads on the ground. The cables will be erased later in post-production. They clicked me into the cables suspended from the high crane above the set and tested how the harness felt as it grabbed me under my ass and thighs, and it felt comfortable. Jamie, another stuntman who

doubles Freddy Rodriguez, was in charge of lifting me up by pulling a cable which he could operate with one hand while standing on the ground about forty feet away at the base of the high crane. He could pull the cable easily with one hand and I would be lifted into the air. Now this is what I meant by I flew. While we were waiting for the lighting and camera to be set up, I would make a motion as if I was preparing to fly, say like Peter Pan or Superman where you outstretch one arm in front of you and make a fist and the other by your side and you bend one knee. Jamie saw me do this and lifted me up and I flew into the air. This was a spontaneous thing, as I had said nothing to Jamie, but when he saw me pretend to take off to fly, he made it happen. It was hilarious and the cast and crew laughed, and when I landed I gave Jamie the thumbs up. This felt great and it really felt like I took off and flew like in a dream, so I did it over and over and each time I did something different like running like Superman and raising both arms into the air in front of me and I left the ground and soared. I was a little sorry when they were ready and we had to stop the flying and shoot.

> "Quentin is about to rape Rose, but he is infected with the zombie juice and his body starts to melt, including his dick, which turns into this long stretched-out, lumpy, squirting thing."

Greg taped my index finger down and applied my bloody severed finger, and on "action," I bend down to retrieve the ring from Carlos's severed arm and the zombie/sicko/stuntman grabbed me, lifted me up and turned me upside down, and threw me into the waiting stuntman, but somehow I got whacked in the left eye. I told the stuntman and it didn't happen again for seven more takes. I also asked the set medic for some Dramamine before we did this as I didn't want to get sick and hurl on the cast and crew below me. This worked out really well and Robert was satisfied and we moved on.

The rest of the scene is after I hit the car and land on the ground. I see the ring about five feet away and have to crawl to it and pick it up, but when I go to place the ring on my finger, of course, my finger is gone, so I get pissed and say "fuck," put it hastily on my middle finger, and look around for the fucking zombie/sicko who did this to me and pull out my gun. I see him approach me, so I punch him in the stomach and chest with my gun, each time firing the gun, and his back explodes twice from my shots. If you've been following these journals, you know we already shot that scene but Robert wants to do it over again because the first time it was too light as the sun was coming up. We did about nine takes of this, and each time, I hurled myself backwards onto the ground as if I had just hit the police car and did my crawl toward the ring. Between each take, Gino would touch up the blood on my finger and splash more blood on my face. My eyes were burning and I thought it was from the handy wipes I was using to keep the blood off my hands and ring so they weren't sticky.

Between set ups I was sitting in my personal director's chair (yes, there is a chair with my name on it), and at three o'clock in the morning they brought out this buffet of sushi. I don't eat sushi but I was so amazed that they brought sushi out to the set that I ate about four helpings and I have no idea what I was eating.

The sun was coming up, so they wrapped me and Freddy, and once I wiped off all the blood and changed my clothes, we were driven back to the hotel. My eyes were really burning at this point and when I got back to my suite and took out my contact lenses, they were dyed red.

Journal Thirteen:

Last night was a blast....literally. I mean, I got to finally blast the zombie/sicko that hurtles me thirty feet into a police car. We shot it before— a month and a half ago— but Robert said he couldn't cut it because it was too light out and the squibs went off too late. I told him I'm glad we were shooting it over again because I hadn't been through the harness flying and ring finding (see: previous journal entry), and now that it is fresh in my mind, I should really be pissed off when that zombie/sicko approaches me.

In fact, I told him, "I should be looking for that next fucking zombie/sicko to show up: how about if I just grab him and yell *you mother fucker!* as I punch and shoot him?" Robert said, "Go ahead."

So, I got to relax a bit while they shot other stuff, and Greg applied my severed finger and spattered my face with blood for continuity, and they called me to the set to set up the shot. Tim, the stuntman who I blast, showed up with two explosive squibs on his back and a hard breastplate on his stomach and chest for when I hit him with the gun, and we rehearsed the action for the cameras. After a little "move to the left a bit more Tom" and "you too Tim," they drew chalk outlines around our feet so we knew the placement, and then our stand-ins took over while they lit the scene.

While I was waiting I tried to think of some emotional equivalent in my life that I could use to be really pissed off, and the first thing that came to my

153

mind was when I was a kid, like in grade school, and casually strolled down to the local recreation center in my neighborhood one summer night. The usual local crowd of teenagers was there, including lots of my friends, and I saw a guy I liked but we weren't close friends or anything named Steve Fisher standing over by the fence, and I went over to say hi. I didn't know it but he was very drunk and as I approached him, he slapped me so hard in the face my ears rang. I was in total shock as my friends saw him do it and it embarrassed the hell out of me. I couldn't understand why he did it because I didn't and hadn't ever done anything to him to provoke it. I just had to think he was drunk and didn't know what he was doing. He's a big guy, and I just walked home confused, but ever since then, I played out dozens of scenarios of what I should have done. You know, I could have punched him right back in his face, but he probably wouldn't have felt it, or kicked him in his balls or something...anything but just walk home with my face hurting and my ears ringing.

So, last night, I imagined Tim the stuntman was Steve Fisher and he just slapped me and I was finally going to do what I should

"I got to scream into the night sky, 'YOU MOTHER FUCKER!'"

have done. In acting class, this would classify as Sense Memory. I am crouching down on the ground as a continuation from what we shot Friday and what I already told you about in the previous journal. I have just put my wedding ring on my middle finger because my index finger has been bitten off, I've pulled out my police revolver, and on "ACTION" from Robert, I stand up, and here comes Tim. I yell, "You Mother!" and smash my revolver into his stomach, and the explosive squib on his back behind his stomach shoots out a big blob of methylcellulose slime and fake blood. I draw back again and yell, "Fucker!" and drive my revolver into his chest, and the squib behind his upper chest blows out an even bigger blob of red goo, and then I just scream and upper-cut him in

the face with my gun, and he spits out about a quart of blood. All the time I was imagining him to be Steve Fisher. You know... it was a summer night, the moon was full, and I felt like I expunged all those pent up feelings I had of that childhood memory. Acting is wonderful.

We all huddled around the video monitors to watch the scene, and technically, it was great; Robert said, "You have the greatest angry facial expressions." Sense Memory: you see, it works, but he wanted to shoot the uppercut again as they didn't catch the blood spitting from Tim's mouth, so we did just that part again and on the second take, some of the blood hit me in the face. It was like bloodlust: I went apeshit and held onto that emotion as Robert wanted to shoot wild lines of just my yelling. That means there is no action, just the boom man holding the microphone near you to cleanly capture the dialogue.

I got to scream into the night sky, "YOU MOTHER FUCKER!" and it echoed across the countryside. How many times do you get to do THAT?

Journal Fourteen:

I had a very interesting, slightly scary morning. There's this girl in San Antonio named Stephanie that I was seeing five years ago and haven't seen since. We've emailed over the years, almost met in Mexico, discussed boyfriends and girlfriends and almost hooked up a couple of times, but it never happened. Even when I first got here in March, I called her in San Antonio and asked her to come visit me, but she had a boyfriend and wanted to come, but he was extremely jealous and she knew if she came, it would be awkward because we've always had a healthy sex life together and she didn't want to cheat on him. Well, just a couple of weeks ago, I heard from her: she broke up with that boyfriend and wanted to see me. I invited her up to spend last weekend with me, and she came and it was just great. She looked great, and we went to dinner with the KNB crew and they all liked her. We had lots of laughs; we went to a nightclub with everyone, and some of the cast from the movie came and we were lounging on a breezy rooftop with palm trees and wide cushioned couches with big pillows, and laying around and talking and cavorting, and she was a hit with everyone.

Last night, I went to San Antonio to spend the night with her, and I got there just after she got home from work and we leaped on each other and…to say the least, we worked up an appetite…and then we went to dinner. We talked about how much we both have changed. I used to be mean and make her cry, and I had no memory of some of the stuff she told me I did. She admitted that she was a bit too possessive and a little bit of a control freak but since being off the pill she has mellowed. She is very nice to look at and sexy and I really was enjoying just being with her. We got home and she put on some great music and did something no one has ever done with me. She conducted what she called extreme foreplay. Don't worry: I'm not going into the details, but I have a whole new respect for giving a woman complete control. It was the most exciting and sexy hour and a half of anticipation to sexy music and mutual appreciation I have ever experienced and when it culminated in the ultimate end, it was explosive and volcanic and the anxiety made it the most exciting thing to happen to me in a long time. I told her she taught me something and I think she is wonderful.

When I got up and left the next morning, two of the tires on my car were flat. Well, not my car— the rental car the movie company provided me with. I thought they were just flat because some neighborhood pranksters let the air out. I didn't want her to be late for work, so I put a can of Fix-a-flat into them and followed her slowly to the nearest gas station. I was driving on the rims by the time we got there and had to sign autographs for the attendant, who was making more of a fuss over me than helping me or getting me more Fix-a-flat. Lucky for me, there was this nice guy named Rick who drove me to Pep Boys and then another garage to see about getting the tires fixed.

The second place had a jolly manager named Joe who said when his crew arrives at eight, he would send someone with jacks to lift the car, remove the tires, and fix them and bring them back to me. That was about forty five minutes from then so Rick took me back to the car and now the tires were off the rims and lost their seal, so I thought while we were waiting, I'd jack up the car, get the weight off one tire at a time, and put some air in to reseal the tire to the rims. I jacked up one tire at a time and put in some more Fix-a-flat and put some air in the tires, but it all

"I know where you live."

came out of two exactly similar stabs in both tires. During the night someone had slashed them.

I called Stephanie and she was sure it was her ex-boyfriend. She broke up with him because he was insanely jealous. He lives down the street from her, so he must have seen us or stalked the house while we were there and this really pissed me off. Now I have to buy two new tires and Joe sent someone to pick them up, and while I am sitting there, I am thinking of how to deal with this jack-off who stabbed my tires. I found out from Stephanie that he worked at Meineke Muffler, that I would pass the place on my way home, and that his name is Billy, and I'm thinking, do I go there and hand him the receipt and say "Hey, this is what you owe me for slashing my tires," or do I go there and tell his manager, "Hey I need to take a photo of Billy over there for the police"? Then I'm thinking I need to hit him where it will hurt him the most, his ego, and I want him to know that slashing my tires meant absolutely nothing to me so I wrote him a note and sealed it into an envelope with his name on it.

When Joe finished putting the tires on I left and went right to Meineke Muffler. I pulled in, and I guess I was going to look for a nametag that said Billy, or avoid anyone with a nametag that said Billy and get someone else to hand him the note. Hey — I'm working on a movie down here: I can't have someone rearrange my face for me or get in any trouble. There was this guy working on a car in the lot, and I went inside and pretended to ask for directions. After these two guys, nametags said Kevin and Ernie, gave me the directions, I said, "Is Billy here today?" They said, "That's him, outside working on that car." I took out the envelope and said, "Will you give him this please?" Ernie took it and I didn't wait for a response, and I got in my car and drove over to Billy and rolled my window down. His back was to me and I yelled "Hey Billy!" He turned, and I said, "I know where you live." He said, "What's that?" I looked right at him and yelled, "I know where you live," and I drove away. In the rearview mirror I saw him go inside. What he read when he opened the letter is, *Billy, It was worth the trouble you caused me by slashing my tires because I got to fuck Stephanie all night.* I put a smiley face there and signed it *Tom.*

Journal Fifteen:

Tonight was an early call and I am supposed to die. This was the earliest call ever as they are trying to get as much done as possible. There's a lot scheduled and the sun was still shining when they picked me up at the hotel. This is a first. Got to the set around 6:30 PM and Greg had already informed Robert and the producers that I must die tonight, as it is the last thing on Greg's schedule and he must fly home tomorrow, Wednesday, to keep the plans he made with his family. We are off Wednesday, and if we don't do it tonight, Tuesday, Greg would have to stay and kill me Thursday. It was iffy all the way, and even the call sheet, the schedule of events, listed my death to continue on Thursday.

Gino is already scheduled to leave tomorrow, and Greg has already packed his room and is ready to travel. There is a lot we have to shoot tonight leading up to my death, which we are shooting in the studio on the JT's Barbecue Shack set, with the crew scheduled to leave in the middle of all this to shoot something on the airport runway outside the studio. Not a good sign as anything can happen when they are outside. We can't just set up and shoot my death as continuity is important and we have to shoot in chronological order.

> "Tonight was an early call and I am supposed to die."

I was hanging around the set, and I heard Robert tell Michael that he decided who would shoot him accidentally. If you remember from a previous journal, we are charging up the hill at the exterior location of JT's Barbecue Shack, after deputizing the town's folk, and Michael as the sheriff tells them to be careful and above all, "don't shoot me." Robert told Michael he would be shot accidentally by Tolo... me. I burst out laughing and Robert turned and didn't realize I was there and we shared sporadic bursts of laughter. You know, the kind where there is silence and you are thinking about it and just laugh out of reflex. He added a line where Michael says "I warned everyone not to shoot me and I never thought it would be you, TOLO!"

This sounded funny but turned very serious the way we shot it. Freddy and I drag Michael into the burning Barbecue Shack, there are flames and townspeople running around and major chaos, and Michael is bleeding from his throat and you think he's going to die. All I could think about was if this really happened how sorry I would be. In my actor's preparation I had already made Michael my brother-in-law married to my sister and established myself as his protector. "So I'm thinking how on Earth am I going to tell my sister I just accidentally shot her husband, and how I fucked up so badly protecting the sheriff.

So, we rehearsed, and I really wanted my reaction to be genuine, so using the "Method" I tried to remember anything similar in my life I could relate to. Immediately, I thought of when I lived in North Carolina and was rushing to work in the morning and got in my car and backed up and heard the little dog named Hamlet belonging to the little boy next door, whom I adored, yelp and run into the yard. It was more than a yelp: it was a dog scream. I had run over him I got out and ran to the dog and so did little Jimmy Reese, the boy next door. When we got to Hamlet, he was standing up and panting and we thought nothing serious had happened to him.

Then his back legs collapsed under him and slowly, he sort of laid down, and Jimmy and I started crying when he stopped breathing and died. It was an accident and Jimmy knew that, but nevertheless, it devastated me.

As I looked down on Michael bleeding from the throat, among the chaos of the set on fire and people running around, I pictured little Hamlet collapsing and on "Action," out of me came a very real and sympathetic "I'm sorry...I'm so sorry" to Michael and to Freddy. We cut to later on as Freddy starts to bandage Michaels throat and I am handing out guns to the townspeople and we have to get out of the Barbecue Shack as it is on fire, and in their scene Michael gives Freddy his gun and I'm supposed to scream "NO...you're not...not to him." I imagined that I gave Michael the gun for Christmas and he promised it to me if anything ever happened to him, and it gave my line some added meaning.

Everyone runs out the Barbecue Shack and as I am leaving, Robert wanted me to casually take out my gun and turn as I hear something outside the window. This was the preparation for the four zombified stuntmen who will eventually crash through the boarded up window, with flames raging from below, and as best as I can fight them and shoot them they overpower me and wrestle me down on a table top and tear me apart. It took them a while to prep the window and build a ramp to it so the stuntmen could run up the ramp and into the window. Greg and his guys zombified the stuntmen and no one has ever seen zombies like this before. They looked like a cross between the Elephant Man and Jabba the Hutt. Their faces were all distorted and misshapen and lumpy and swollen, and they had huge slimy humps on their backs protruding from their torn shirts, and their arms were thick and pitted.

The first shot was of me in the foreground turned toward the window and flames were everywhere, and the first guy was supposed to come in and take me out of frame, and in a new camera set up, we'd shoot the rest of the fight. Once they got me down on the table, the only thing left that involved me was lying on the table with explosive blood packs on my chest and legs so as they pull on me, the blood explodes out of me. The rest happens to the fake body Greg had prepared to come apart at the legs, as one arm is ripped off and my head and arm and part of my chest is torn away from my body. He built a remote control head that looked very much like me: its tongue could dart in and out, the eyebrows could furrow, and the mouth could open and close as if I was still screaming.

So, the first stuntman comes in and I use his momentum and hurl him across the Shack's countertop, and the second zombie comes in and I hit him in the face with my pistol at the same time, firing. The back of his head blows out, and as I point my gun to the other zombies, one grabs my arm and the others grab my legs and wrestle me to the table as I scream and fight. We did that about five times and they called "lunch." It is midnight and all that is left now after lunch is for me to lie on the table and have the squibs, explosive blood packs, explode and I am done. The rest is the fake body being pulled apart. We are all still worried about getting to that as the crew will pack up and head out to the runway right after lunch for however long that shooting will take.

I wiped off all the slime on my hands from fighting the zombies and went to lunch and hung out as usual at Greg's table with his crew of artists.

"Then his back legs collapsed under him and slowly, he sort of laid down, and Jimmy and I started crying when he stopped breathing and died."

157

After that we waited...and we waited...and we waited...and I was on the empty set exchanging makeup artist stories with Eric, one of the artists on Greg's crew. Every now and then I asked him what time it was and we figured out, "okay if they come back at three, that means they won't start shooting again until four, and if all goes well with the explosive packs, you guys can rig the body by five and we really will have killed me, and Greg and I can go home tomorrow." So, we smoked cigarettes and told stories and time was going by, and almost like a jump cut in a movie, the crew was back and I was fitted into the extra set of my wardrobe that had the explosive squibs rigged.

Greg reapplied all the blood that was on the other costume and since we knew this was my last scene he just piled the blood on.

I could see he was enjoying just slapping this sticky shit all over me and I didn't really care as I knew this was the last time. I didn't opt for padding under the costume to protect me from the impact of the squibs. I didn't think there would be any, but with the costume on, I could see the squibs were very close to my face and I was worried they would explode into my face. So, I suggested that as I am struggling with the zombies I would have my head raised up, which fit well with the camera that was pointed straight at me and the table and the zombies, and when I screamed and put my head back, that would be the cue to explode the squibs, and that is what we did. There was also an overhead camera that showed my entire body. The first take was it. I screamed, the explosions went off, and all I felt was like someone hit my leg with a hammer. That was the only one I felt. Then I was really covered in blood and it was running beneath my clothes and every time I took a step, my clothes stuck to me all over. I hate that feeling and told Greg he should be happy that I'm sticky all over.

I stood around like that for a while and soon I was called to the set so Greg and Gino could match the blood on me to the fake body now on the table. It was a very strange feeling I wasn't expecting when I got on the set, and Greg and his crew were working on my fake body. It was

> "No one has ever seen anything like this in a movie."

odd to see myself lying there with the guys working on me, and my head is tilted back with a screaming expression. When they were ready on "Action," the zombies pulled on me and my legs and one arm came off in a bloody flesh-stretching mess, and there was a slight delay and my arm chest and wriggling head came off, stretching muscle, and the tendons snapped as it dropped on the floor. The crew applauded and the girls screamed, and I could now go take a hot shower. The assistant director brought me some sweatpants, shampoo, and a clean t-shirt and I took the greatest hot shower of my life because I felt so sticky and the hot water felt so good until I heard a noise and saw movement, and Greg burst in with a large basin filled with ice cold water and threw it on me. It didn't feel bad though, as the overwhelming thought I had was "Awww...he cares." I laughed while I scrubbed.

I went back and sat with the cast huddled around the video monitors in our own chairs with our names on them, fully expecting Brian to announce, "That is a picture wrap on Tom Savini," but he came over and said, "There is another scene we need you for on Thursday which is you firing your gun at zombies and then you'll be wrapped okay?" Of course it would be okay, as every day on this thing has been a blast.

Journal Sixteen:

It was un-fucking believable, and shocking, and stupefying, and jolted us into screaming fits of joy and amazement I thought tonight was going to be another slow, boring, "Let's get these last little bits of scenes shot" kind of night. It started out that way when after hours of waiting in the miserably hot sound-stage/airport-hangar with sticky blood applied to my face and shirt, I was called onto the set to follow Michael, Freddy, Jeff, and Rose through the meat locker in JT's Barbecue Shack into the back storage room where he kept "the escape vehicles."

I was in the background for the whole scene and when we watched video playback, you kind of saw a little bit of my elbow behind Michael and that was it. Is this what they kept me for, and why I am going to have to stay until next week? This, on a Friday, after my glorious death scene on Tuesday and months of shooting, was how I was going to spend the rest of the shoot?

This weekend off, then return Monday and Tuesday as planned to be in the background and maybe just maybe get to be featured shooting some zombie/sickos when they attack the Barbecue Shack?

Greg and Gino have gone home and so have most of the people I was hanging out with. It is so hot now that we are inside the studio and shooting in the daytime that Emmy, the gorgeous brunette playing my sister, collapsed from the heat on the enclosed set and had to have her feet wrapped in cold towels and be given oxygen. Between takes they turn on the air-conditioning that blows out of a huge yellow directional hose, but unless you are in its path you still have to fan yourself with the nearest makeshift fan like a script or call sheet.

I had accepted this fate when they called lunch and I slowly walked the hundred heat-soaked yards to the trailer area and catering tent. I loosened my uniform tie and collar and took off my shirt and was in no rush to where it was really too hot to eat, but this was purely routine behavior...to go to lunch when it is called. I got a light salad and was sitting in the tent with the costume department when Brian announced that Marlee had arranged for a Ben and Jerry's Ice Cream truck to show up and give us free ice cream. Michael Parks was "picture wrapped" and we applauded his goodbye from *Grindhouse*, and after lunch, Robert was going to show us the six minute preview he's put together for the San Diego Comic-Con this weekend that he, Quentin, Marlee, and Rose would attend to promote our movie.

Now we're talking. This would be exciting; however, I didn't expect it to do what it did. Inside the same sound-stage/airport-hangar we were shooting in, all of us leads sat close to the monitors and there were huge speakers set up on either side. The rest of the cast and crew sat in director's chairs and stood in a huge semicircle facing the monitors. Robert gave a little speech about the purpose of such a preview and how when they did it for *Sin City* it created quite the internet buzz.

"Then a white screen appeared and you heard my voice screaming, "SHUT THE FUCK UP!"

Robert pressed a button and an old time movie theater logo for "previews of coming attractions" that we were used to seeing in theaters twenty years ago came up, followed by projected film blemishes like scratch lines and, burns, and film-jumping, then a tombstone surrounded by flames that then lit the front revealing *R.I.P.* engraved in the stone. Titles beneath it appeared, reading "Rodriguez International Pictures Presents." We all laughed and applauded this direct homage to American International Pictures and what you would have seen when you went to a Grindhouse theater.

Then a white screen appeared and you heard my voice screaming "SHUT THE FUCK UP."

It was my line and then the police station scene comes up; I come in and my finger has been bitten off. Robert is opening the preview with that scene all the way until when Michael hears some distant growling and turns to it and says, "Is that him?" Then all hell breaks loose in the following montage of images. It's hard to remember the order so I'm just recalling what I saw:

Rose as a stripper on stage looking sexy and fantastic and strutting her stuff

Explosions and zombies walking down a hospital corridor looking diseased and slimy

Freddy runs up a wall and flips to the floor and fights and kills zombies with Jackie Chan acrobatics

I am thrown into the side of a police car

Rose in a hospital bed crying because she is missing a leg

Freddy breaks a leg off a table and snaps it onto her stump

Rose walks down the hospital corridor and her right leg is gone, replaced by a table leg

Danny Trejo from *Dusk Till Dawn* in a phony preview where he plays "Machete"

A Jacuzzi with large-breasted women with "black tape optical effect" across their nipples

Cut to Danny slamming a helicopter machine gun turret onto his motorcycle, and he and his bike are flying through the air out of a huge ball of flame and the flames give his devil face a fiery red and orange glow as his machine gun blasts pointed flames at us

Cut to low angle of him opening his floor length coat and there must be 25 machetes in the lining and a huge title appears *MACHETE: Avenger of death* or something like that.

Titles appear saying "Starring:" and our faces pop up on the screen like they did in old films and our names are under them. Freddy tells Rose, "I have a present for ya," and attaches a machine gun/rocket launcher onto Rose's stump, and we see him spinning out on his motorcycle with Rose on the back spinning toward us in slow motion as Rose blasts zombies with her leg and they explode and spatter blood, another ball of flame and Rose is flying through the air in front of it and when she lands she fires a rocket from her leg at an approaching car and it flips out of control coming right at her— she rolls away just in time.

Zombies tear people apart and the most disgusting parts are covered again by the "black tape optical effect." Cars crash, windshields break, infected zombie blood spatters, eyes stare, zombies march, the crazy babysitter twins smash a car with sledgehammers and slam to the ground when the car pulls away, Quentin as soldier rapist screams and melts, heads are blown off, people are dismembered, zombies are blown to bits, and then the title *Grindhouse* travels across the screen, and at this point, everyone in the sound stage is screaming and applauding and no lie, this went on for a full five minutes. My heart and everyone else's was pounding, and the overwhelming feeling was we wanted to see more. No one has ever seen anything like this in a movie. This is going to be very big, and the buzz will start and when people see this, they're going to have anxiety attacks until it comes out.

I hugged Robert and told him the world isn't ready for this movie, but I think of it now, and I think the world has been waiting for this kind of movie, especially the fans. It was what we all needed. The film is winding down, and we want to go home and the preview was a punch of adrenaline, a buzz that got us high on what we've accomplished together.... of what we just saw, of what the world is going to see. The San Diego ComicCon is going to have an injection of *Grindhouse* right into the demographic that will come to see this movie.

I settled in again not caring how hot it was, or what tedious scenes were left to shoot, and cast members and crew who weren't around at the beginning were coming up to me with thumbs up declaring how great they thought the opening scene of the preview was, and I went on about how Freddy is going to become the new action hero, and Brian called me to the set along with the still photographer.

Once we were on the set he said to everyone, "It is my extreme pleasure to bid a good night and that is a picture wrap for Deputy Tolo and Tom Savini." The cast and crew burst into applause and I had to fight bursting into tears. What a surprise. I thought I would have to continue next week, and now I can go home freshly buzzed from seeing the preview.

Robert signaled me to come close so the photographer could get a shot of me and him together and he asked me to raise my hand, and my bloody finger missing stump, into the shot. I can't remember who the many hugs came from in the blur of my watering eyes as props removed my pistol belt and gun and handed me the back of my own personal director's chair that I used for the entire film, with the word *Grindhouse* printed on one side and on the other side, my name.

160

Machete Journal

If you've seen *Grindhouse*, you know it's a double feature of two movies, *Planet Terror*, directed by Robert Rodriguez and *Death Proof*, directed by Quentin Tarantino, and some outrageous fake previews and fake movie trailers sandwiched between these two features. One of these fake trailers was for a pretend movie titled *Machete*. This trailer became very popular and there seemed to be a collective desire for this movie to be made. It's been two years now since *Grindhouse* and that movie is finally being made...and I'm in it. Yay! I play Osiris Amanpour, a vile, loathsome hired killer, hired to kill Machete... played by old *From Dusk Till Dawn* nemesis Danny Trejo.

I'm in Austin, Texas again at the hotel they've put me in and I went down the gift shop to get a pen and off the elevator comes Danny Trejo... Machete. You would recognize him instantly. He has that kind of face, the face you've seen so many times in villainous roles like in *Heat* or *Desperado*... weathered and tough, and the kind of face on a person who does not take any crap, who is scary... and he is going to kill the shit out of me, at least in the script, and to make up for what I did to him in *From Dusk Till Dawn*.

I stabbed him in the heart with a broken pool stick, causing him as vampire to disintegrate and melt away in flames while his eyeballs rolled into the corner pockets.

That's how this adventure down here started. I emailed Robert Rodriguez, the director, and said

"Danny should kill me, don't ya think, as sort of a comeuppance for me killing him?" Robert wrote back, "Rad." So we started emailing back and forth with photos and ideas on how I would look, and since I would be a "specialty" killer, the question was... what would be my specialty? I told him not to forget I am good with a bull-whip and throwing knives and tomahawks and that I am also very good at archery. He liked the archery idea and asked me to send him some photos with a bow. There's a scene in the film where the villain is looking at videos on the computer for hired assassins and mine is a video of me in action with a bow.

I got the phone call on Sunday, and I had to be here in Austin shooting on Tuesday. What? Holy shit! What a scramble to get shit together and pack without knowing how long I would be there but I did it and they flew me down first class (Screen Actors Guild rules), and soon I was in Austin, in the wardrobe trailer trying on black jeans, a black wife-beater, leather jacket and bandana and being led to the set by Nina Proctor, the costume designer, for Robert's approval. It was dark and very hot on the green screen stage. Danny Trejo and Jessica Alba were sitting in a car doing a scene while a technician rocked the car every few seconds with a large 2 x 6 plank under the back bumper on an apple box as sort of a homemade fulcrum.

Robert smiled at me, and I could tell, as usual, he was thinking many thoughts at the same time, and in between those thoughts, he moved me into better lighting, checked me up and down, and gave a thumbs-up to Nina. Nina said she would sew some silver studs into the sides of my jeans, and I was happy for that and to be dressed in black and leather because the last time I was here doing a movie with Robert, I was dressed in tight police uniform kha-kis. This is more me.

Now, after having the driver assigned to me, Chrissie, take me to Whole Foods to stock up on grocer-ies, I am checking into the hotel and asked if there was the usu-al refrigerator in the room and they said no, just two beds and a TV, and they apologized for having to put me in a smoking room. I said, "Well, I have these groceries." The clerk said, "Let me see what I can do," and I was led up to a private access floor and entered my new room. I thought they made a mistake. I walk in and gasped.

There was a huge, and I mean really huge, living room, big-ger than two com-bined floors at my house, with two large couch-es, a big desk, a big screen television, and a bar sink, two big bedrooms with a king bed in each, a laundry room with washer and dryer, and two walk-in closets. It scared me. I couldn't believe it. I unpacked, put the groceries away and went for a walk. Around then corner from the ho-tel on Congress Avenue was a movie theater called The Paramount showing *The Mummy*:

Boris Karloff's *Mummy* and *The Black Cat* with Karloff and Bela Lugosi. Now I am convinced that somewhere between leaving my house in Pittsburgh and coming here that I died and am now in Heaven.

I, of course, bought a ticket, went in and sat down hypnotized by a Sylvester and Speedy Gonzales car-toon actually playing on a movie screen in a very decorative movie theater still surviving and boast-ing a summer old film festival. I felt like I had traveled back in time to my life as a kid in the fif-ties. I went back the next night to see *Alien 3* and *Aliens*. I ducked out in the middle of *Alien 3* and walked the six blocks to the famous bridge in Austin where thousands of bats fly out from under the bridge at dusk, but it was 8:30 and they had flown out at 8:15. I'll catch them another night. I went back to the theater and continued *Alien 3*, then *Aliens*. I'm looking forward to the weekend and the double feature of *Day The Earth Stood Still* and *The Forbidden Planet*. Heaven.

The next day, my first day of shooting, I was rehears-ing on a sound stage where they've built the interior of a church with the altar, pews, a large empty crucifix, big stained glass windows and big wooden entrance doors. Robert rehearses me and three stunt guys, including Aaron Norris, the son of Chuck Norris, who I haven't see since *Invasion USA*, in a scene where I come in looking for the Padre, Cheech Marin…because I want to kill him. We establish the blocking, carrying rub-ber weapons, then I am taken to the gun handler who wants to familiarize me with the weapon I will really be using: a big, heavy Russian USAS automatic shotgun. Yes. A shotgun machine gun. I've never seen or heard of anything like it. The gun handler told me when they test fired it in Los Angeles, they were handcuffed and arrested: there were helicopters, and it closed down the bay area for hours. We were in the back of an equipment truck and he fired it first. The world shook. Awesome. Then it was my turn and I put the sling over my shoulder, locked the handle under my right arm, and using only one hand, pulled the trigger. How can I possibly describe the feeling of a machine gun blasting twenty-two shotgun shells down the length of this truck? It was the most powerful feeling I've ever had.

We did the scene in the church over and over. Then stunt guys fired their weapons across the altar as the Padre is running past, and I fired this awesome Earth-mover. I really enjoyed the last two takes. During the first few, I was in character, thinking, "fucking priest," but for the last two, I was just enjoying shooting this canon. The muzzle flash had to be at least eight feet long. Aaron and Norm, the two stunt guys in front of me told me they could see the flash blast between them.

While they set up the squibs on the altar for the gunfire blasting out the statues and splintering the wood, I sat with Cheech and talked with him for over an hour and a half. At first, I didn't want to bother him sitting there but he kept asking me questions that turned into the conversation. Somewhere in the middle of this, they shot the sc ene and set off the squibs, blasting the altar into chunks.

Cheech and I talked about so many things. He was getting married in two days to his Russian girlfriend of five years, Natasha. We talked about Vlad The Impaler, women, makeup effects, and Tommy Chong and their Australian tour, and it was such a joy to be sitting there with a guy whose comedy albums were so much of my pot-drenched brain and life in the late 60s and early 70s. Then we did the scene where I crucify him to the altar cross.

Earlier I shot him in the leg and dragged him to the altar. After I nailed his right wrist to the cross, he has a scene with Jeff Fahey, who nails his left wrist to the cross. I'm sure there will be protests somewhere.

The next day I was hanging out by the stainless steel pool on the roof of the hotel and these two guys started up a conversation with me. They said they were street musicians traveling from Seattle down to New Orleans and they were stopping here before heading up to Washington, D.C.. They said they were driving an old truck that got towed, and they got really nervous when security showed up on the roof, and I was wondering how they got up on the roof as it was private access. We talked about a lot of things, and one of them recognized me and even knew my name. Soon room service arrived with food they had ordered but when the server asked for their room number to bill the order to, there was no such room and no such name attached. One of them sort of sneaked away while the server called down to check on another room number they gave him, saying they couldn't remember the room as they had just gotten in. The other guy shook my hand, and said, "nice meeting you," and he sort of ....dissapeared through another door.

Later that night, I was coming out of a music store and they both walked by carrying a drum, a guitar, and a dog on a leash. I pointed at them and we all recognized each other and they asked to take a photo with me. Afterward, I gave them 20 bucks and said I kind of figured what they were doing on the roof. They said, "You gotta do what you gotta do."

It's Sunday today and I've been on hold since Thursday and decided to stay in Austin and not fly home. This morning I walked into the gym and Danny Trejo was there working out. We talked for a bit and he said he, his kids, and Jessica Alba had gone out to the clubs on 6th street the night before. He said people wanted his photo and he was like, "Hey look: it's Jessica Alba— she's right here. Why do you want MY photo?" He said TMZ stopped him on the street and asked about his divorce, asking, "What are irreconcilable differences?" He said, "I had a great wife and I was stuck on 'stupid.'"

I was on call to do a scene with Jeff Fahey at his house/office where he is having with the killers he has hired to kill Machete. I was picked up at the hotel and driven about an hour to a type of place I'd never seen before. It was like a housing compound, a community of houses like you might see in *Back to the Future* but these....after going through these huge King Kong gates it was a community of ... mansions. Every one a big sprawling multi-floored, multi-layered well....mansion, palace, castle. I've never seen so many big beautiful houses one after a glorious another, the next one bigger and more beautiful than the one before.

We stopped at one that had its own King Kong gate and pulled up to the 28 million dollar house of the guy who invented PayPal and designed microchips for Dell. This house took my breath away. I was flabbergasted, flummoxed, and gobsmacked. It was like walking into the Vatican or a big city museum. Everywhere I looked, there was enormous glorious splendor. After walking through the front door, which was a huge, double-arched steel gothic, heavy boldly-designed thing, I was under monstrous marble pillars that supported an expansive white dome that was painted ala Michelangelo with classic biblical figures: hand-painted obviously by someone or a team on a high scaffold.

The library rivaled the Carnegie Library in my neighborhood. The pool table was something you hiked to in the middle of a huge room where a huge couch faced a wall of stock market monitors surrounding a huge built in television screen. The couch was U-shaped but a huge U about the size of half a city block. On either end, instead of having arm rests, there were two leather love seats, all part of the couch.

Off that room was a home theater. A gigantic screen and whole room looked like it was made of red velvet, and instead of theater seats, there were long red velvet couches covered in an array of colorful pillows and cushions.

This house had a profound effect on me... that people live like this.... that they have to go on long walks to get to other sections and I didn't even see the upstairs. It affected me so much, I couldn't speak when I had to deliver my lines to Jeff Fahey, who sat behind a huge desk in the library. I forgot and couldn't remember from moment to moment the only three lines I had. I had to pull myself together... had to get motivated... had to get into character. It kind of worked from minute to minute, but I felt as if I'd blown it, that I said my lines half-heartedly and wasn't really feeling it or meaning it. I'm hoping it comes across as some idiosyncrasy in the character. We'll see. The scene involved all the assassins sitting in front of Jeff Fahey's desk and he's asking, "Machete... Machete...what the hell kind of name is Machete?" and I say something like when you spend your life killing, you kind of take on the name of your favorite weapon. Rose McGowen then says to me, "Then how come your name isn't DICK?" I pull out my own huge switchblade that I brought with me to the set and put it on my crotch and press the button. It opens with torque like a big shiny metallic dick to shut her up. She later plays an assassin who carries a cat around petting it, then shoots her victims through the cat (killing the cat too, of course).

A couple of weeks have gone by. I flew home and spent time with James and Lia. Lia said she would feel miserable when her friends go to Las Vegas and she can't go, so I financed a trip for her and James to go to Universal Studios in Florida for a very long week-

> "When you spend your life killing, you kind of take on the name of your favorite weapon."

end. She got a new job, nine-to-five on her feet, and she starts when she gets back.

I enjoyed my boat, camping, the archery range... and I was thinking about what the script said about Jeff Fahey scouring the internet for videos of hired killers and coming across my site 1-800-HITMAN and how it changed in the new script to a scene where they are only looking at photos of hired killers. I called my best friend Rob Lucas, who is a D.P., (director of photography) and we decided that since they cut the idea of "killer video resumes" in the script, perhaps because of the time it would take to shoot such a thing, that I would create one here in Pittsburgh, and Rob would shoot it.

I printed photos of Danny Trejo and backed them with cardboard, and took them to a fir-

ing range and an archery range. In the video I arrive on my motorcycle with a bow slung over my shoulder, and soon I am pulling back on an arrow and let it fly at a red balloon. When the arrow pops the balloon, it pierces Danny's photo in the middle of his face. Then you see me raising this awesome pistol, a Contender which fires a 30/30 rifle shell, and aim it at Danny's photo, and I fire and a huge hole appears in Danny's forehead. I intercut this stuff with me working out in the gym and doing my famous "hardly no man can do this pushup" pushup, and lifting weights, all greased up and voila: I have a resume video of an assassin/killer.

Now I am back in Texas. I was picked up at the airport and taken to the production office to get my per diem and pick up my rental car. Robert was shooting this big battle scene on the backlot with all these jacked up cars and Mexicans with all kinds of weapons. This movie is going to look big. I grabbed Archos with the killer video Rob and I made and headed toward Robert and the video village where he watches the shots. A big guy, who I thought was Robert's cousin, walked up to me and grabbed my hand and started shaking it and telling me what a fan he has been his whole life and had my books. He introduced himself with,

"I'm Nimrod." Boing! This guy is the director of Robert's next movie, *Predators*. I said, "Oh... you're Nimrod!" because I had heard of him as the director Robert had picked for *Predators*. During a break in the filming, Nimrod was saying to Robert and pointing at me, saying, "This is THE MAN!" We took photos together and it seemed like a perfect opportunity to show Robert the video right there in front of Nimrod. Robert loved it and said it would be in the film, and he would put it in his computer and instantly thought about how he would use it by putting it in multiple screens as they look at killer resumes.

Over the next few hours, I hung out with Nimrod and he showed me all the wonderful stuff he was preparing for *Predators*. It looks amazing from all the sketches and models and paintings on the walls. He talked about the characters, and I'm not much of a schmoozer, but I threw in, "any need for an older Italian guy?" He said he would love it but it would have to be approved all over the place and if not in *Predators,* he said we WILL work together. He called me his rock star, and as I left, he yelled, "Ladies and gentleman, Savini has left the building!" We all had dinner together later: me, Nimrod, and his wife and child.

We did a scene yesterday when my thugs and I approach the church, a real church, where I kill Cheech. The scene we already shot on a set of the church interior. Here we are, five of us carrying these big guns into this real church... and there were real worshippers inside, not extras. I wondered what would happen if they turned around and saw us coming in carrying these guns, and I said that to Norm, one of the thugs and a cigar-smoking buddy. He said, "Maybe they would think their prayers have been answered."

Today I was in the gym on the recumbent bike, and my mind was wandering and I thought of the love scene coming up with Danny Trejo and Jessica Alba. After my workout, I was heading back to my room, and Danny was in the lobby saying goodbye to some of his cronies who were visiting him, and one of them told me, "Hey...last night he kissed Jessica Alba." Danny said, "She was a real trouper," smiling. Later, I saw Danny and his boys getting off the elevator, and I asked them if they've seen the tabloids today. Danny said, "No...why?" I told him they say that Jessica Alba has left her husband and child and is running away with Danny Trejo. He cracked up and gave me a high five.

Been hanging around Austin, working out, lying by the pool, shopping, and now in two days, my big death scene is scheduled where I have to fight a bunch of Danny's guys before they overpower me and kill me. I'm really nervous about it. I've never been in a fight, a real fight. Every time I say that, people think it's unbelievable, especially people around here. Lots of tough guys and stuntmen. And I've never had a bunch of guys grab me... big guys... except in grade school, a bunch of guys grabbed me once, and one of them started punching me. They held my arms and feet and kept yelling, "Hit him in the face," but he kept hitting me in the stomach, and then they let me go. From that day on, I started learning about self-defense but I never had to use it I guess I could use that experience here, but this is a lot more serious. I killed Danny's/Machete's brother. I crucified him to a cross in his church, and now they have captured me and are going to kill me in the Chop

Shop. You know: a motorcycle and auto shop. Lots of sharp tools and saws and stuff.

I'm nervous about it, even though my philosophy has been, learn the lines and when you're there, use the situation and believe it and have fun seeing what come out. But, I've never killed anyone that I know of, even in Vietnam with all that firing into the woods. It was possible but one on one, eye to eye, killing someone? I've not done it and I'm supposed to be this hired killer. Experienced. I have to come across brutal, hard, bad. It's just not me. Friends who know me will tell you I'm a pussycat. A teddy bear. It's going to take a lot of technique to be believable. I have to believe it…. in close up. That's what makes me nervous.

Went to dinner with Nimrod at one of Robert's favorite Mexican restaurants: La Fonde… something. I told him "Nimrod" no longer conjures up the meaning "dolt" to me. He laughed, as he apologized to the waitress seeing the word "Nimrod" on his credit card. I meant it. We laughed and had some great conversations about movies and philosophy. I had a watermelon margarita and we laughed so hard and so voraciously I don't even remember eating the food. When he dropped me off at my hotel, he came up for a bit and after more conversation, I gave him my *Most Dangerous Game* script because when we talked he said *Predators*, that he is directing, is a lot like that famous story.

We didn't shoot my last big death scene on Friday, and it is now Monday when we were supposed to shoot it, and they are saying it will be Wednesday. I'm really starting to get homesick now, as I've been here two weeks and only worked one day. I'm running out of things to do, so I went out and bought a new phone. A Blackberry. I figured learning to use it will keep me occupied. It has.

Aha… they called. I shoot the death scene and finish up tomorrow, Tuesday, and not Wednesday. I go home on Wednesday. I don't think I've been very good in this part. I could be wrong. I'm counting on the way I look and just being technically ominous to make the role believable because I just didn't feel it, and today I'm scared. I'm a killer about to be killed.

How do I react to that? Am I bold and brazen with the attitude of *fuck you… bring it on*? Am I scared and wimp out… how do you play being killed?

The day has come. Today we shoot my death scene. I don't know how I am to be killed but it's something to do with a saw.

> "I don't know how I am to be killed but it's something to do with a saw."

I am sitting in my trailer and I'm trying to get into character… I'm in killer mode and a fly lands on my knee so, as the killer, I should be able to catch that fly in my hand… you know… lightning reflexes and all. I didn't catch it but at least I'm thinking like a killer or am starting to.

I decided not to sit in my trailer all day and went to the set. It is a big parking lot with a steel structure named "Machete's Chop Shop." This is where all the low rider cars they advertised for and got will come rolling out on cue. I've never seen such souped-up, individually interesting homemade cars.

My first scene is me sitting in a car and talking on the phone to Jeff Fahey (Booth), telling him I found the Padre. There is a red Ford Focus sitting there as my car but Robert doesn't like it and says for someone to bring his car around. Soon they drive up a BMW Roadster Z4 just like mine, just like the one I just bought back home except Robert's is black. It was red but it got some hail damage and he had it painted flat black. It looked great. Unique. I did the scene and was anxious for it to be over so I could get out and tell Robert that I have one of these. When the scene was over, I grabbed my new Blackberry phone and couldn't remember how to pull up photos of my car. I finally figured it out and showed it to him before "the moment" fizzled.

They called lunch and told me I could stay in my trailer as they were not going to need me for a while. A long time went by: the whole rest of the day actually. I spent the whole time agonizing on whether I would be convincing as someone being killed. Will I act defiant as the script says, or like a wimp and beg and cry? I have to know this so I can prepare my mind properly. I have a couple of lines to Danny like, "you don't expect me to cry like your cry-baby brother do ya?"

How is that going to come out? Then I say, "wait... I'll talk, I'll tell ya where Booth is. He's the one you want." I imagine I'll say it calmly and laugh but like, *ha ha...okay then (you guys win)... I'll talk* as if there is no threat... and my death is like... whoops! we killed him... but I really don't know how I'm going to do it.

They call me to set, and the first thing is a bunch of big guys and a couple of guys my size have to drag me into the Chop Shop. I'm glad it wound up being five big guys because I'm not going to make it easy for them to get me in there, and I'm really going to struggle. They did it first with a stunt guy playing me to show me the action, and he kind of went through then motions... acting like he was struggling. They put me in there and called *action* and they couldn't get me in, let alone move me, so they grabbed my legs and added guys and carried me in, and on the way in, I threw the guy my size all over the place. He was tripping and falling and being thrown left and right. I really, really was struggling hard and violently. We did three takes and each time they braced themselves for a real struggle, and it was very real. Then they set up for killing me and the assistant director did something very unusual.

Usually AFTER your final scene, he announces to the cast and crew that "it's a wrap" on whoever the actor is, and you get some applause for your work in front of them for the shoot. This time he did it BEFORE my last scene. "Ladies and gentleman the next scene will be Tom Savini's final scene in the film and he is wrapped." This surprised me and got some polite applause, and now I am really nervous and anxious. I'm taken to a metal table and I don't see a saw blade anywhere near it so I'm thinking maybe they are going to CGI it in later. In the meantime, Robert comes over to me and says, "just say your final line and change it to *you don't think I'm gonna talk like your crybaby brother do ya?*" Then he pauses and says, "No: go ahead and say the whole thing." Now there is all this talk about how I

> "Will I act defiant as the script says, or like a wimp and beg and cry?"

am going to be covered in blood. This is right after the photographer said when the scene is over he'd like to do an on-camera interview with me, and someone else is telling me my flight home is very early the next morning.

If you've read any of my other journals, you know I just fucking hate fake blood. It's sticky, it stinks, and the worst part of it is it stains. I now have visions of flying home with red hair and ears and blotches all over me, not to mention being covered in blood for the *Machete* interview. Then Robert told me there would be no blood, at least not on me, and that he intends to show the actual action of my death by focusing on Danny's face and his watching it happen, as well as on the other actors standing there.

I am lying on the steel table and they give me a pie plate to look at next to the camera as my focus, my eye line to speak to Danny. I have to say it loudly as it is very noisy in the Chop Shop with welding sparks flying in then air behind me. A big guy throws me back onto the table and in the middle of my first line, Tyler, the prop guy, advances on my face, holding a huge circular saw. It isn't running and the blade is made of rubber, hard rubber, and it's shaped like a real saw with real pointy saw teeth. He is struggling to hold this thing up about a half inch from my face.

Robert calls action, the big guy throws me back on the table, and Tyler starts the saw and the combination of the loud saw noise and the blade so close to my face just scared the living shit out of me. My lines came out loud and totally believable because I really was saying them like a wimped-out pseudo-tough guy begging for his life. It all just came out of me at the last second because of the scene, these mean-looking guys, and that fucking saw. Robert called "Cut," and the whole cast and crew filled up the tin structure with applause and whistles and "Yeah"s. After all my nervous anxiety on how to play the scene, this was certainly worth it.

I had to do it again just for audio, just for the microphone without cameras running. Again, there was applause and Robert came over and hugged me, and we took photos together. I went to do my interview... without blood. Woo Hoo!

Now it's about a year later and the movie has come out and I'm at a convention and fans are coming up to my table and telling me they saw *Machete* and how much they liked it and wondered what happened to me in the movie. I did all this horrible stuff to Machete, and then I just kind of disappear. I hadn't seen the movie yet, and I say no, they kill me in the movie, didn't you see it? The reactions from fans who saw are like, "Oh I must have missed it," to "No man: you don't die in the movie." I rushed out to see it in the theater, and I don't die. There's no death scene. There's no "MY death scene." I called or emailed Robert, I don't remember now, and he said, No man, your character was too cool. I'm bringing you back in *Machete II*."

Ha… great… maybe I get to do a knock-down, drag out fight with Danny.

In the interim, before the movie came out, something really horrible happened. Just before we finished shooting, when Nimrod was giving me the tour of the *Predator* props and renderings, I saw in (and I'm not going to mention his name) a publicity team member's office some publicity photos of me they took during the shoot. I asked if I could have some of them and was told absolutely not. There is a policy of no cameras, no photos to be taken, and no one gets photos or even sees photos until after the movie comes out. Over the course of the next few weeks, I kept hounding him for at least one photo to show my daughter and girlfriend what I was doing on this movie and how I looked. I assured him over and over again the photos were only for me to show my family and girlfriend. I really laid it on as to how I would never dream, never in a thousand years, let the photos out or post them or do anything with them before the movie came out except have them privately in my collection. This publicity team member is just a really nice guy and did me a favor, trusting me; he put some of the photos on a disk for me, and again I assured him there would be no sharing of these photos. He even hand-delivered the disk to my trailer to make sure it was safe.

I took the photos and put all of them in a montage on a single 8x10 photo, and of course showed it to Lia and my girlfriend, and when I went to my next convention I brought it with me as the answer to the often asked question of "What is your latest project?" I would simply show the photo and tell them it is from *Machete*. The convention was Spooky Empire in Orlando, Florida and they have a whole ballroom dedicated to tattoo artists doing tattoos. I decided to get my skull tattoos that I now have on my shoulders, and they took eight hours spread out over two days. On the second day I was sitting there, getting my right shoulder done, and I got an urgent email on my phone from Robert's wife Elizabeth. She asked me why on earth am I showing and posting all over the internet the photos of me as Osiris from *Machete*?.

What?! Fuck! I knew nothing about it. It turns out someone from Bloody Disgusting something or other on the internet had gone to my table lifted the cover I placed there while it was getting my tattoo and took a photo of my MACHETE photo. It was soon posted and was all over the internet. Elizabeth was heartbroken and very angry and very disappointed with me. Then I heard from Robert and he was very disappointed with me and was like, "How could you do this to us?" Then I got a message from the publicity team member that just depressed the hell out of me, that he had trusted me and I had promised him and it seemed like I was running around going, "Hey everyone… look at me… I'm in this new movie *Machete* and aren't I wonderful and don't I look awesome… " and well… it was mortifying.

So, here I am, sitting there getting a tattoo and feeling the pain from that, and feeling the pain of innocently alienating Robert and Elizabeth and the team member, and trying with my left hand on my cell phone to apologize to Robert and Elizabeth and the team member, and trying to get someone I know in the biz to help me get that posting on the internet taken down. I am right-handed so that was a chore.

*"No man, your character was too cool. I'm bringing you back in **Machete II**."*

I finally got my friend Jovanka, who said she knows the site. They did take it down but it was too late. Other sites had posted it and I was doomed.

Elizabeth called again and said the publicity team member's job was on the line and would I call Robert and see what I could do. I called immediately and apologized my ass off and explained how it happened and that it wasn't me showing off and bragging but in fact, the image was stolen by someone photographing it. It really did look that way too on the internet: a copy of a copy. I explained that it was not the team member's fault as I hounded him daily about the photos and promised him upside down and sideways no one would see the photos. I had hounded and hounded and it just really was not his fault and I promised him it would never happen again. In the meantime, I felt like shit.

I sent Robert a beautiful automatic knife in a mini Halliburton case, and I guess he forgave me because after he got it, he sent me a message that said something like, "Savini, you always have the greatest toys. Thanks, bro." Only then did I feel better about the whole thing.

Machete Kills Journal

June 13, 2012

This is only the first day on this movie and so much has happened. To begin with, I am also in the middle of playing a part in Quentin Tarantino's *Django Unchained*. I am on a small break from that movie until I go back to shoot my death scene. Actually, it's the death scene for all the slave trackers and I am one of them, but that's another story for the *Django* journal. They switched the schedule so many times it didn't look like I was going to be able to do *Machete Kills*, but at the last moment, they moved our tracker death scene until later in the month, and that left a window open for me to come down here to Austin and reprise my role from *Machete* as Osiris Amanpour.

The only drawback is that my hair and beard are super long, having had to grow it that way for *Django*, and I have to keep it that way for when I go back. So, I don't look like Osiris Amanpour, but more like a caveman. But Robert Rodrigquez, the genius director of *Machete*, all the *Spy Kids* movies, *From Dusk Till Dawn*, and *Sin City* and many others, said he can work the hair into the story, and by God he did.

I had a 6:45 am call this morning, after getting here quite late last night and I was so tired the room was spinning, but up I was and picked up and taken to

ROBERT RODRIGUEZ'S
MACHETE KILLS

Robert's Troublemaker Studios. I was delivered to Nina, the costume designer, who put me into the best black jeans I've ever worn and some Harley Davidson boots and a black t-shirt with a priest collar.

Yes, I am a priest in this one.

Actually, Osiris Amanpour has changed his ways and is now a priest and very sorry for killing Machete's brother Cheech Marin in the original *Machete*.

I was taken to the set for Robert's approval, and on the way, Danny Trejo (Machete) came out of his trailer, and we hugged and chatted a bit about the last time we saw each other at a horror convention in Germany. I got to the set, and when rehearsal was over, Robert came out, and we hugged and he gave me the up and down and the thumbs up, and we had a great conversation about *Django*; then his trainer Rudy came over, muscles flexing all over the place. Rudy's not a big guy, but a sculpted physique bulging from under a loose t-shirt, and we all had a greatconversation about working out while the company photographer, Rico, snapped away at our posturing and flexing.

"Yes, I am a priest in this one."

171

There was a couple of things in the script I was concerned about and one of them is how I was going to do a "shocked fucking senseless expression when he sees Machete": that's what the script says happens when I see Machete come into the room. I wasn't sure how to pull that off, but Robert started talking about my intro into the scene beginning with that expression. I would be looking through a magnifying glass at some explosive I was working on, and when Machete walks in, it will be a close up of my eyeball getting bigger as I see him enter. Terrific: I can do that. I'm going to suggest that after I do the eyeball in the magnifying glass that I peer over the top of the glass and as you see my mouth made huge by the glass I would mouth the work "fuck."

I went to the makeup trailer and Becky did this terrific contoured makeup on me accenting my cheekbones, darkening my eyebrows, and giving me a tan and it looked so good I shot myself in my trailer mirror and sent it to my daughter Lia and my girlfriend Jodii. Hours went by until Vanessa, the trailer manager, knocked and told me to go to lunch. On the way to lunch, Michelle Rodriguez was coming at me, carrying her lunch back to her trailer, and I said "Hi" and "I am your Osiris," and she gave me the fist-touch handshake and said she remembered from the first *Machete*. I was elated

as I am a fan of hers not just from *Machete*, but from seeing her in *Avatar*. I have a big poster in my bedroom of the *Machete* poster that is just her and her guns and eye patch.

After lunch, it was back to my trailer and I practiced my lines in front of the mirror, and more hours went by, and Vanessa knocked again and Iliana, the producer, was there and came into my trailer. She told me Robert is taking the cast to dinner tonight and got my cell phone number so she could stay in touch with me about it. Shortly after she left, Vanessa knocked again and said they weren't going to get to me today and I could leave. I went right to the hotel and jumped into the great swimming pool there and laid in the sun for about an hour. I left when a loudmouth jerk on a cell phone paced back in forth behind me during his inane conversation. I went back to my room and continued my nap until Iliana left a message that she would pick me and Michelle Rodriguez, also staying at my hotel, up around 8ish.

At 8 o'clock, Iliana texted and said more like 8:30 as they are still shooting, and then she sent a text that she was down in front, waiting in a rental car. I went down and Michelle hadn't shown up, so I went to the front desk and tried to call upstairs to Michelle's room but there is no Michelle registered. I remember a driver saying Danny told Michelle to use a fake name so no one bothers her and she immediately said Betty Crocker. So I asked for the guy to call Betty Crocker's room and there was Michelle. I told her we were waiting and down she came and we went to the best and fanciest Mexican restaurant I've ever seen. I think Robert knows them all.

We went in and were led down a flight of stairs and I had to duck under a low rock ceiling into a room that looked like it was carved out of rock; we were inside a rock cave. Robert's ex wife and producer Elizabeth was there with their children, and so was Danny and other producers and there was a guy I was introduced to named Eli who I learned had just been given a billion dollar contract from NASA. I don't know much more about it but he had a British accent and he was very bright about a lot of things, and we kept hitting him with questions about everything, including time travel and ancient civilizations. I think Robert is using him as some kind of technical consultant, as part of this movie concerns outer space and missiles and a lot of stuff I'm not privy to with the limited "sides" (my portion of the script containing my part) and so I am going to see when I can get my hands on the whole thing.

"I can't imagine anyone wanting to pick a fight with Rudy. He looks like Superman without the costume."

Dinner was amazing with big tamales wrapped in corn husks and chicken soft tacos that tasted the best ever, and soup, and fish, and some amazing corn on the cob that was coated with some kind of cheese and spices. I've never had such great Mexican food. The kids were going from guest to guest and I did some magic for some of them. Robert was constantly taking photos with this big Nikon, and Michelle had engaged Eli into some long explanation about the science of space travel, and this was a whole experience for me with Robert. I am usually so in awe of this man and his talent that I stay quiet and just listen, but tonight it was like we were like old pals and talked a lot about old times and *Dusk till Dawn*. His sister Rebecca, who is the editor on this movie, chimed in and said, "Remember when we decided to not put Tom's (my) death in the original *Machete*?" Robert went off about why he made that decision to avoid constantly cutting away: that's why I was there, not dead, and with a whole new character arc for Osiris.

It was Robert's birthday, and they brought out this wonderful double chocolate cake with action figures on it wearing capes with big "R"s on them, and immediately, Michelle grabbed one of the figures and Robert grabbed the other, and they mock wrestled with them all over the table. Robert put his on a plate and made like his figure was flying all over the place before it would swoop down and attack Michelle's guy, and the kids went crazy with hysterical contagious laughter.

I noticed at one point Rudy, Robert's trainer, had come in, and Robert spoke to him briefly about how he wanted one of the fights to take place. I got the impression Rudy was helping with the choreography.

Later that night, as we were getting into our cars, Rudy came by and said he had just gotten into a fight with some guy and "had to take care of him." He pulled up his shirt and asked me if his back was all scraped up, and he did have this open bloody patch under his rib cage.

I can't imagine anyone wanting to pick a fight with Rudy. He looks like Superman without the costume.

June 15, 2012

Can life get any better? Tonight I got to kill tons of bad guys with Michelle Rodriguez. I had an AK-47 and she had this huge Magnum handgun. Danny, of course, had his machete. The day started off lazy as the call was for tonight at 7:15. I woke up late, rented a bike from the hotel, and did the 10 miles around the lake right behind this hotel, The Four Seasons.

How do you get lost going around a lake? I don't know, but I did. I came off the trail and had no idea where the hotel was. When I found it, I went to the gym and worked out, and then spent the rest of the day trying to find out who my impostor is on Facebook. Someone created a Facebook profile using the exact photo I use and some of my profile. I thought I found out who and reported the whole thing to Facebook and now we'll see what happens.

All of this investigation took place at poolside

at the hotel with me running up to the room to investigate with my computer then back to the pool. I thought of the idiot yesterday who was aggravating the hell out of me with his stupid phone conversation and made sure for all my calls I was far away from people and talked into the shrubbery.

After a short nap, I was picked up and taken to the location, Troublemaker Studios. I was hanging out in my trailer and decided to visit the set to see Amber Herd play Miss San Antonio, then back in the trailer until around three in the morning when we began our scene. It was Danny driving the taco truck from the first *Machete* and me and a guy named Stuttering Tito jumping out of the back of the truck: me with an AK-47 and him with a shotgun. There are a bunch of bad guys everywhere dressed in black suits firing at us.

I don't who anybody is, why they are firing at us, why we are shooting at them, and why the hell there is a Miss San Antonio dressed like she just got off the pageant runway, firing at Michelle Rodriguez and yelling, "My dress cost more than your life" Blam blam blam! I mentioned to one of the producers that I only have my sides to read and I'd like to have the whole script because I don't know who anybody is. Later, when we all finished, a script was sitting on my dressing room table in my trailer.

Michelle wasn't feeling well tonight and twice went to some bushes to try to throw up. Once she went right in front of me and I grabbed my chair and moved away. In a bent-over position she turned and laughed as I walked away, and I just said, "Just trying to give you some privacy." She laughed. It must have been something she ate or something because she felt so much better later when she was able to throw up. She is a real trouper and went whole hog into the scene.

So, we jump out of the back of the truck and I peer around the corner and then fire a few rounds at the scattered bad guys. We weren't really firing:

"It's a big mistake as an actor to try and memorize HOW you will say something in a scene."

we were mocking it, and they will CGI the muzzle fire later. But I keep going... *pffffoough*... I fire like you do when you're a kid and I had to stop doing that for the sound takes. Tito runs around the corner toward the bad guys and I yell, "no wait" and he is mowed down.

Michelle marches right after him, blasting away and pulling him around the back of the truck while I give her cover fire. Danny comes around the corner and gets into the truck using my shoulder to get in, and I jump up to pull the door down. Michelle asks me how many bad guys are left and I gave her the Quentin Tarantino *Inglorious Basterds'* German number three hand sign. Robert picked up on that. The truck pulls away and we continue to blast the bad guys. And that was a wrap.

June 17, 2012

I read the script. Oh my god...this will be amazing. People are not expecting THIS.

June 18, 2012

Boy oh boy... I earned my pay today. Danny Trejo tried to kill me but Michelle Rodriguez stopped him... in the story of course. I've been really worried about a scene I have with Danny. He needs a bomb expert and when he asks Michelle's character if she knows one she says yes, "but you don't like him."

She takes him to meet the bomb expert and when they walk in, he is behind a huge magnifying glass and all you see is his big eyeball magnified in the lens. It gets bigger when Danny walks in and the bomb expert sees him coming. This is the way Robert set up the introduction of me as the bomb expert.

I am still Osiris Amanpour from the first *Machete*, and if you remember, I killed Cheech Marin, Machete's brother, who is a priest, by crucifying him to a cross in his own church. I now have to convince Machete that I have become a good guy and want to fight on his side. Well, of course, as soon as Danny comes into the room and recognizes me, he jumps me and starts to strangle me, and all the time Michelle is reminding him that he needs a bomb expert. Danny lets me go for a moment and I reveal that I am now a priest and want to right the wrong

I committed against him when I killed his brother.

Anywayyy... what I'm worried about is that I am thinking in order to be convincing, I have to cry when I tell him, "I know you would prefer to see me all sorts of dead. God has already cursed me for what I did to your brother... and please have mercy and I swear I will make it up to you." I have been storing up all my sorrow and keeping it in for days leading up to this scene, and my worry was, will it be there when I need it?

It's a big mistake as an actor to try and memorize HOW you will say something in a scene.

You must just memorize the words and when you're in the scene, believe your situation and feelings and get into it and the words will come out as they should in the context of the scene. So, my main concern was that the scene NEEDED FOR ME TO CRY TO CONVINCE MACHETE THAT I HAVE CHANGED. After all, I killed his brother, so I have to really mean it.

The priest collar helps but I am in a tight black t-shirt with my tattooed arms exposed, and Danny is strangling me and on one take, I grabbed his upper arm, and on the next take Danny asked me not to grab his arm as he wants his bicep to show bulging when he strangles me. I understood this completely because every time I hold a gun or do something physical I am also trying to show off my biceps. It's called using your instrument.

So, today is the day and of course every angle was shot in the scene EXCEPT the angle on me for my speech to Danny. I am holding back and holding back and saying the speech over and over again for Michelle's angle then Danny's angle and then the master shot, and finally, the angle is on me and it's time.... and Voila'... it came... the real sorrow... the real tears... the real crying as I say my speech.

"I spent the day with Mel Gibson. Ha... I know: it was awesome."

The shot was over, and I expected out of the thick silence that enveloped the set that there would be applause, or some kind of "whew... that was great Tom... wow." Robert did come over and tell me "good stuff" but instantly went into "Okay... do the beginning a little faster and string it all together with a little less emotion and make sure you pronounce all the words clearly." I did it over and over again, crying every time for the camera and realized THAT is why I am there: to act. And, being that emotional on that level is what acting is all about. I was doing just that. I was proud of myself, and today I really felt like an actor.

Just to be a boring Twitter-like, I-think-everything-I say-is-important-Facebook-jerk, when I woke up this morning, my watch was still set from how the continuity people set it on location last night. So, my watch said 10 o'clock and I decided not to rent my daily bike and go on the ten mile dirt trail behind the hotel around the lake, because check out time is noon and that's when I get picked up to go to the airport.

But when I looked at my phone it said 7:30 so I decided to get a bike and do the lake one last time. Of course today, the day I have to get on a plane and go enjoy a few days of summer at home, my bike skidded on some rocks and I tore a big hole in the palm of my hand, scraped my shin bone so it looks like it took a shotgun blast, and scraped the skin off my right forearm. I did NOT scrape off the tattoo of my daughter's name there on my arm. Whew.

175

I go home today, and a few days later, I go to New Orleans to continue shooting *Django*, but that's another journal. Then I'll come back down here around July 11.

July 11, 2012

I spent the day with Mel Gibson. Ha... I know: it was awesome.

He walked past me as I was sitting in my "Osiris" labeled director's chair and said, "Hey Dude,... how are ya?" You have to understand I don't give a shit what they've said about him on the news because it's none of my business, and it's none of their business. This is the guy who gave us *Braveheart* and *Mad Max* and *The Road Warrior*, and one of the best horror movies of all time, *The Passion Of The Christ*. He was a riot today. He kept doing some of my favorite bits, like walking up to people and pretending to trip and spill an empty glass on them, and walking into things. He was very friendly with everyone and spoke to me a few times, once about his new shoes that were giving him lots of pain, and once about the previous *Machete* that he had seen. He's playing the American version of Richard Branson who is a billionaire toying with space travel.

This movie is not about the Mexican border problem but it's really a Bond movie, full of gadgets and technology... and outer space. The more I hear about it, the more amazed I am. I saw Danny Trejo's embryo clone in a large vial and was told it fights another embryo clone, and Danny, playing two parts, also fights his life-sized clone. Michelle Rodriguez is frozen in carbonite and not in the Harrison Ford pose, but giving the finger.

I did a scene with Danny in a bar fight where he clobbers this bad guy with his rifle butt and spins him to me, and I clobber him again with my rifle butt.

"That's fucking Mel Gibson: we have to get a photo with him."

July 12, 2012

Not only did I get to hang out with Mel Gibson today, but I did a scene with him and Danny Trejo, and Mel actually shoots me dead with a ray gun that turns me inside out. What? Yep. All true. Life is but a dream.

The day started typically with pick up at the hotel and to the location, an abandoned Home Depot, and then costume and makeup, and then to the set. The abandoned Home Depot is huge and Robert has many sets built inside: a nightclub, a sort of Star Wars interior with tons of gadgets and ray guns, and a trophy room that floored me, as they were setting it up with suits of armor and swords and daggers, and it took my breath away. Anyone who knows me knows what a sword and armor freak I am, as every wall in my house and studio and gym has swords and daggers all over it.

We sat in the video monitor area where the director's chairs with our character names printed on them sit in front of monitors where you can watch what is happening on the set.

Today we are continuing the previous night's scene where Danny and I run out of the mad scientist's party and look for the beating heart that will somehow destroy the world if it stops beating.

We find the beating heart and I am supposed to be the explosive expert who can disarm it, but I look at it and tell Danny something like, "High octane organs ain't my bag." The heart and the electronic housing keeping it alive explodes, and we look up and Mel has shot it. We confront him and he grabs a different weapon and points it at Danny, and I step in front of him to protect him, and Mel shoots me square in the chest. I spin around and tell Danny "Were even," and I sort of implode and turn inside out. I don't know what that is going to look like and I am looking forward to seeing the effect.

Danny did a great thing in between takes when he turned to me and said, "That's fucking Mel Gibson: we have to get a photo with him."

I instantly grabbed my phone out of my pocket. Danny grabbed me and we walked over to Mel and Robert and Danny just said we are getting a photo with you and Mel. He handed my phone to someone and they took the photo. I instantly searched my phone photos for the photo of the stairway leading into my basement computer room that has a life size photo of Mel as William Wallace from *Braveheart* permanently attached to the wall. I showed it to Danny and he brought me over to Mel and made me show it to him. I told him that the photo was on the wall leading to my computer room and he said, "What? Some guy with a skirt?"

Later, between takes, as Danny and I were hovering over the electronic beating heart and exchanging jokes, and I said, "Danny where does your lap go when you stand up?" He thought for a moment and said "Thighland." For some reason, at that moment, it was hilarious and we laughed out loud and did the fist connect. No one has ever had an answer to that question. We told Big Craig, Danny's right hand man, the joke and he said, "what's the capitol of Thailand?" Danny said, "What," and Craig whacked him in the balls and said, "Bangkok."

Later on, between takes, I asked Mel if I could ask him a question about *Apocalypto* and he said sure, so I asked him how he did the decapitated body falling down the long stairway in the beheading scene atop the Mayan-like temple. He said he just used a skinny stunt guy and put a padded body suit on him and a green motorcycle helmet, and the guy took the fall down the padded steps. Danny chimed in with how great the scene and the effect was.

I was told I had one more shot to do and when I got to the set, Brian, the first A.D., announced to the cast and crew that "This is a good night and a picture wrap for Tom Savini." There was applause and I yelled "thank you!" to everyone, punched the air, and did a full spin right into shaking Robert's hand and thanking him. He opened an envelope and pulled out a lobby card he had made featuring me in a good pose featuring my tattoos and the printed *Machete Kills* logo. Then he opened another package and gave me tequila in a sort of Cinco de Mayo skull and he and Danny and I posed for photos holding all this stuff. I hugged Danny and

told him I loved him, and I left the set and was driven to the hotel, reliving every moment of the day. I felt so good about what we had done and the scenes I was in and sent a text to Robert that said, "Hey man, just want to say how grateful I am to you and everyone else who has been so fabulous on this project. What a feeling. I am deeply touched, and I wish you the absolute best with all my love." He wrote back, "U were awesome and another glorious death and awesome role. Thanks for doing it. Made it super cool. Seeing you and Danny face to face with a James Bond set and beating heart was geek heaven."

Unbelievable.

I was going to end this chapter with the last paragraph above, but I am still in the hotel here in Austin, and I just went down to the gym and walked in and heard a familiar voice say "Hey dude," and when I turned, it was Mel Gibson. I just worked out with Mel Gibson, and he was amazed that I am sixty-five and look this fit. We talked about many things, and he showed me some Chinese breathing exercises, and I showed him some oblique exercises with dumbbells that he thought really worked and he felt it. He is fifty-six and was doing some really strenuous stuff with heavy weights and high intensity pull-ups and in general doing a full body workout.

My day is made. I worked out with Mel Gibson.

Ted Neeley, James Parks and David Steen

Django Unchained Journal

I am in New Orleans right now, acting in the new Quentin Tarantino movie *Django Unchained*. It is his first Western, and I am playing a slave tracker named Tracker Stew.

I arrived here on Tuesday, April 3rd in New Orleans with my girlfriend Jodii, and right from the airport, I was taken to Academy Award nominee Sharon Davis for my costume fitting. It is a period movie taking place in the 1850's, so I was wearing pants and the boots I felt the most comfortable in and a baggy shirt and then the piece de resistance, a fur vest made of raccoon skins with the head placed right in the front of my chest. I immediately decided to use the raccoon, to think of the raccoon, as an ex-pet that one of the slaves, D'artangan, has killed in a drunken rage. I am to sic three of the most vicious shepherd dogs onto him in one scene and now I have a subtext, something to think about while in character while siccing the dogs on him, something to hate him for. Roy, our driver, explained to us that the huge drainage pipes we are seeing on the side of the highway were built a year before Katrina hit down here because New Orleans is like a bowl that water pours into from the Gulf, and there is no natural drainage. The problem is the generators for the drainage pipes were built on ground level and flooded out from Katrina and they couldn't turn them on, therefore, there was much flooding. He also explained the joy of eating crawfish, something I haven't tried yet.

Later that day, we went to the French Quarter and I bought some cigars from a place where ten guys were sitting there rolling the cigars fresh in front of us, and I ate a Muffaletta sandwich. Don't ask me what was in it, but it's a local favorite and it was damn good. People all around us were eating crawfish, as it is the crawfish festival season.

That night, we joined some of the KNB crew at a local bar/restaurant around the corner from the hotel and waited for my friend Gino Crognale to arrive from the airport and join us. It was me, Jodii, Jeff Edwards, Carrie Jones, and Big Jake, and the bar was so unnecessarily loud, it felt like we were at a rock concert and it was so hard to hear anyone talk. I hated it. When we left, Jake made a remark about my character being named Chaney.

"What?" I said. "No my character is Tracker Stew." He said no, and didn't I know that Quentin changed it to Chaney? I thought he was fucking with me but he brought up the cast list on his iPhone and right next to my name it said Tracker Chaney. I was floored and very emotional thinking how thoughtful it was of Quentin to change my character name to reflect the biggest influence of my life, Lon Chaney. That is Quentin. He knows everything, and is such a gracious guy.

Wednesday, April 4th

We were driven to the location, a real plantation about an hour from the hotel. We met and drove with one of the other Trackers, James Parks, the son of the fabulous Michael Parks, who was the Sheriff Earl McGraw in *From Dusk Till Dawn* and had the similar role in *Grindhouse* and *Kill Bill*, and who surprised the hell out of me playing Escabar in *Kill Bill*.

We arrived at the plantation and it was a circus with all the tents and trailers typical of a location shoot. We got into our costumes and slogged around in the mud. It had been thunderstorming all night and the weather down here has been causing havoc with the schedule. In fact, I am supposed to leave here next Wednesday to fly to Austin, Texas to be in *Machete Kills*, the sequel to *Machete*, and to play the lead of a motorcycle gang in a video game also to be shot there, and I am wondering at this point if I will make it there.

They formed this massive arch with enormous branches reaching across the road from both sides, and the hanging moss gave it a real Southern countryside feeling. This feeling was solidified and validated by seeing Jamie Foxx, on horseback, wearing his slick gunfighter outfit, leading a group of slaves toward Quentin Tarantino, who was behind the camera, riding a huge sweeping crane on a dolly tracking them.

Between takes, Jamie was constantly practicing drawing his gun and twirling it and flipping it effortlessly back into his holster.

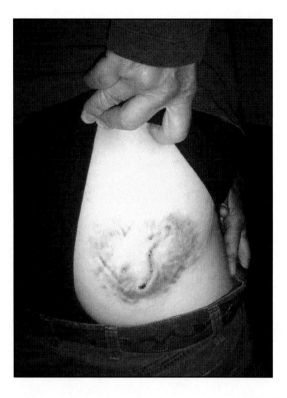

I haven't seen Quentin since the Premiere of *Grindhouse* in downtown L.A. a few years ago, and I have since then grown to respect and admire him ever more after seeing *Inglorious Basterds*. Here he is, dressed entirely in black and wearing a cowboy hat and riding the long arm of that crane, and even though he started shooting *Django* in November and it is now the beginning of April, he is still enthusiastically enjoying every minute of what he is doing, laughing and joking with the crew and when the shot is over, he comes over to us standing on the side of the road.

He greeted James first, then he came over and shook my hand and said how great my costume looked, and spun me around and hugged me from behind and said,

"And you don't look Italian... thank God."

I came around and took his hand and shook it and thanked him for changing my character's name to Chaney. He tipped his cowboy hat to me and said, "aha... see... I knew you would like that." I told him I loved it. He liked our costumes and we bid him goodbye until tomorrow, when we would be shooting the beginning of the Tracker stuff.

After we got out of our costumes and got back into

"And you don't look Italian... thank God."

the van to take us back to the hotel, Greg, the second A.D., came over and said tomorrow, Thursday, there is a change of plans. Because of a bad weather forecast, we are simply going to the sound stages so Quentin can see all the Trackers at once in costume, and we will begin the Trackers stuff on Monday. Now I'm really wondering if I will make it on time to Austin, but I really don't care. This film is the all-important project right now.

I passed a trailer and saw a taped name on the door. Freddie Hice. Freddie was my stunt double in 1980 in the movie *Knightriders*. I can't wait to see him.

That night, Jodii and I went to Bourbon Street and it was a cacophony of hustlers and bands, and food and booze, and voodoo shops and masks, and balconies and bright lights, and we can't wait to go back on Friday night with the boys. We are off Friday and Saturday and Easter Sunday.

Thursday April 5th
Woke up and went to the gym. It's a great gym, and at 10:30, I went down to the van waiting to take us to the sound stages less than a mile away. James Parks was there, and soon Robert Carradine was there and I introduced myself to him and a guy named Dave Steen, and Ted, and the driver told us we had to wait for one more, a guy named Mike. We waited 15 minutes, and Mike showed up and said, "Sorry guys: that's the last time that will happen," and then he said, "I smell like a French whorehouse." I said, "Why, did you go to one last night?" and he said, "No, I couldn't find one."

At the sound stages we were just in time for a test of the dogs attacking a stunt double for the actor playing D'Artagnan. There were three dogs, big, vicious-looking Belgian Malinois Shepherds and they are trained to attack the stunt pads the stunt man was wearing, and of all the dogs in creation, they have the strongest bite pressure. On *action* they just tore into him, latching onto the pads and clothing and pulled and tore and dragged him about 15 feet. The trainer yelled at them to stop and two did, but the other one just kept tearing at the stunt man until the trainer made him stop. It was really scary and me and some of the other guys remarked how vicious that was, and oh my god— imagine what a tiger or lion would do.

I was standing with the other Trackers and suddenly realized who the guy named Ted was. He was Ted Neely, the guy who played Jesus Christ in the movie musical *Jesus Christ Superstar*. Like the biggest geek fan, I walked over to him and said, "You're Ted Neely" and took his hand and shook it and said, "Man, I enjoyed the hell out of you in *Superstar*."

Luckily, he appreciated my compliment and often in the day would come over and start conversations with me as to what he has been doing or about the dogs.

We all got into our own trailers and put our costumes on and reported to the outside of one of the sound stages where Tom, the prop man, handed us our own sheathed magnificent bowie knives. I have quite the collection of knives at home and the one he handed me was a really nice one.

Inside the sound stage was a huge replica of the plantation house. It was magnificent with its huge pillars and the interior was amazing with many floors and completely furnished. Quentin came out and greeted us individually and made a few comments about how fabulous we look and what a bunch of killers he would not want to be around. I joked he was going to out-Peckinpaw Peckinpaw and he liked that and agreed, and he physically showed us how we were going to die in one of the end sequences when Django kills all of us.

He was on the floor showing how Dave was going to get his balls blown off before Django kills the guy behind him.

"One of the few things I'm stealing from the original Django," he said. Dave's throat is cut and his head chopped off and split in half and put into the stew pot. "Out-Peckinpaw Peckinpaw?"

The script says I am cleaning my gun and when Django appears and starts killing everyone; I try to put my gun back together and just before I do, Django shoots me in the head, but here at this little meeting it seems it is up in the air as to who is doing it, and I think Quentin is giving it to Robert Carradine, who is a Tracker with a hump on his back. I asked if he knew any lines from *Richard III* and he instantly went into a monologue from it.

Quentin loved how we looked. We all left and Monday is now when we start the Tracker stuff. Our call is 5:30 am.

Friday April 6th

We woke up late and headed to the French Quarter and tried to get a Mint Julep, thinking this is part of the culture down here in the South, but two bars, including one in a swanky hotel called The Carousel where the whole bar and stools rotated with a huge lighted carousel awning above us, couldn't make us one because they didn't have any mint. Finally, we went to a little dive bar and the bartender had mint but didn't know how to make it unless we told her what is in it. I suggested she look in her bar manual and she found it, followed the directions, and made us two Mint Juleps. I slugged mine down like soda pop.

Later that night we hooked up with Gino, Big Jake, Jeff, and Carey Jones and went walking on Bourbon Street, which was full of hustlers, voodoo shops, bar after bar, strip club after strip club, band after band, and tons of people, drunk, sober, begging, dancing, yelling, singing, wearing costumes, and it was the most festive street you'll ever see. We went to LaFitte's, the oldest bar in America. It started in 1772 as a blacksmith shop that served drinks and it is now just the bar lit entirely by candlelight. I ordered Chartreuse on the rocks. Now, I don't drink. I am not a drinker. I never started. It wasn't important to me and I

"A tank rolled over me, Kamikaze planes crashed into me..."

saw what it did to other people and have no interest in it. In fact, I hate drunks, especially drunk women. BUT... this is New Orleans, and I joined the crowd and I was the designated walker as every one else got drunk as skunks as they say.

Saturday April 7th

Everyone stayed in, nursing their hangovers, and I went to the World War II museum and then next door to the Tom Hanks/Steven Spielberg 4-D giant screen presentation on World War II. I sat down in front of the biggest movie screen I've ever seen, other than the Omnimax in my hometown of Pittsburgh. When the movie was over, I felt like I had just been through the war.

A tank rolled over me, Kamikaze planes crashed into me, and it actually physically snowed on me and the audience. After that I left, lit a cigar, and went for a very long walk. Bliss.

Went back to the hotel and just lazily laid around watching television and ordered a movie from the hotel, *Tinker, Tailor, Soldier, Spy*. Excellent.

Sunday April 8th: Easter

Easter Sunday we woke up late and went to a screening Quentin set up at a local movie theater of an Indonesian film called *The Raid, Redemption*. It was the most brutal, violent film I've ever seen, and I've made a lot of them. Quentin was there in the front row, laughing his ass off, really not just watching the movie... but you could tell he was studying it. Very inspirational. Samuel Jackson was there in the audience sitting behind us and occasionally yelling out, "Yep, that's what I would do."

Outside the theater, Quentin and I talked about *Hunger Games* being a total rip off of *Battle Royale*. He asked if I had seen the photo on the internet of John Travolta and Sam Jackson in the car scene from *Pulp Fiction* with the caption "What do they call *Hunger Games* in France? *Battle Royale* with cheese."

> "I asked for the dogs and I got the dogs, and at the end of the day, Dave and I will have to go to the hospital and get tetanus shots."

Later that night I played *Lord of the Rings* from my iPod to the hotel television for Jodii. She had never seen it before.

Monday April 9th

We are picked up at the hotel at 5:30 am and taken to the set. It's at a swamp but we are delivered to our trailers just off the highway near a dirt road leading to the swamp. I get into costume with the rest of the Trackers: Dave Steen, Ted Neeley, James Parks, Robert Carradine, Mike (never learned his last name) and a few others who I never quite met. The ones I mentioned became our little clique, especially me and James and Dave. Robert had a hump on his back as part of his costume and character, and all day, whenever somebody said anything about his hump he said, "What hump? (A la *Young Frankenstein*. Get it?)

We were hanging out on set outside the Tracker hut, a rather spacious kind of bunkhouse that would be where we lived on the plantation. It had bunks and a huge stone fireplace, a wood stove, and a table and some crude chairs, and would be where we are all killed later on in the movie on the rebuilt interior on a sound stage sometime in the middle of May.

Leonardo DiCaprio arrived on the set and came over and introduced himself to us, and I didn't realize it until later when I saw his performance that he introduced himself to us... in character. He is playing the leader, the head, the master of the plantation as a fragile, but tough as nails Southern aristocratic gentleman slavemaster, and that is how he had introduced himself to us.

I am very impressed with Leonardo DiCaprio. One. he is one of the most beautiful men I've ever seen. Forget him on screen. In person, he is stunning, gorgeous, extremely good looking. I kept staring at him when he was talking to us, and I really felt like kissing him.

183

I AM NOT GAY, but I had the same feeling that you get when talking to a beautiful woman. It was the beauty that was attractive and his manner. There is a reason people like him are movie stars. And on set, he would be there, off camera for someone else's close up and be a hundred percent THERE for them. He would be in character and doing it in full out performance mode all day for them. This is when he is not even on camera but doing it for the other performers, even down to the least featured characters.

When the camera WAS on him, he was amazing: varying his performance and giving a wide variety of deliveries take after take. This is a true movie star and professional.

I asked for the dogs and I got the dogs, and at the end of the day, Dave and I will have to go to the hospital and get tetanus shots.

Quentin wanted to see who would be good with the attack dogs. I mentioned to him that I wanted to be one of the Trackers who cared for and trained and handled the dogs. They sent me and James and Dave to work with the dog trainers, a really lovely lady named Tamira, her husband, and Tom Roach, a young trainer who worked with me. He brought out Bullet, an older dog, ten years old, and this dog was smart and had talent. Tom said "left side" and Bullet rolled over onto his left side. Tom said "right side," and Bullet rolled over onto his right side. Tom said, "stand, sit, beg, lie down, hit your mark" and Bullet did everything he said. Tom put a dog treat on Bullet's nose, and Bullet just sat there looking at it until Tom said "get it," and Bullet would flip it in the air and catch it in his mouth.

Tom handed me Bullet's leash and said he was going to put Bullet in "Agitated mode" and it was up to me to hold onto him. He told me to brace myself and showed me how to hold the leash; he gave Bullet a little hand sig-

nal and the dog went berserk, barking and yelping and jumping up and advancing on Tom's position. It was like holding back a car... HE WAS GOING TO GET TO TOM... and I was just a hanger on.

Tom showed me where to put my hand, holding the loop at the end of the leash sort of behind me against the side of my waist and bending my legs, and that really helped me center myself and made it harder for Bullet to pull me but I'm telling you...it was a workout. I worked with Bullet for a while and pretty soon, I was leading him around and forcing him to go where I wanted to go. Tom said, "Just go where you want to go with confidence and the dog would feel it and go with you. Pull on his leash but don't tug on it because that makes him think you want him to attack. Be forceful with words like 'Stay,' and 'Come with me,' and 'Mark,' for making him stay on his mark, and 'Leave it,' when you want him to not play." I got really comfortable with Bullet and it looked like he was my dog and I had been with him a long time.

When we got to the set, me and James and Dave were to have the dogs in "Agitated mode," holding them back and away from a runaway slave who climbed a tree to get away from the dogs. The head trainer thought it would be a better match for some reason if I had one of the younger dogs named Hank and took Bullet and gave him to Dave. I didn't know Hank, hadn't worked with him, and he seemed a lot more rambunctious. The trainers hid near the tree and gave a the signal and all three dogs went insane, barking and yelping and trying to climb the tree, and running in circles and running at the tree again. Ato, the young black actor playing the escaped slave D'Artagnan, was up in the tree acting suitably scared.

On the way to the set, a handsome cowboy on a most gorgeous horse called out my name. It was Freddie Hice. He looked great. He was tanned and healthy and hadn't changed since 1980. We talked later about that experience and how he was hurt when they cabled off a motorcycle he was riding as me in the film; his thigh bones had slammed into the handle bars, and almost every stuntman on that movie got hurt. On the last day of the last stunt after two stuntmen did a "cable off," the stunt men jumped up, checked themselves over, saw they did not have any broken fingers or collarbones, and screamed with joy.

Soon, a gorgeous fancy carriage being pulled by a really beautiful and huge Clydesdale horse, and carrying Leonardo and Christoph Waltz, the Academy Award winning German actor who played that amazing Nazi in Quentin's *Inglorious Basterds*, pulls into the scene. Leonardo has some words with D'Artagnan, reprimanding him for running away and saying he paid five hundred dollars for him and he expects five fights. He tells us to shut those damn dogs up so he can think, and Dave hands me back Bullet and I take Bullet and Hank out of the scene.

We did this over and over again, and on one take, I heard Dave yelling, like he did in most of the takes, but this time it was different. He was sort of screaming, "FUCK!!" and when I turned to look, he was being attacked by the other two dogs.

One dog had bit him square on the ass tearing off his pant and pulling him down to the ground, and Bullet was making a beeline for his throat. Just as Dave put up his hand to protect himself from Bullet, the trainers ran in and calmed the dogs down.

> "When I turned to look, he was being attacked by the other two dogs."

Dave was upset and kept saying he was bit. The first A.D. called "Lunch." We all left and were taken to lunch at a catering camp just off the highway down the road. We just let them take care of Dave. After lunch, we saw Dave and he said he had holes in his butt and when we wrapped shooting, he would have to go get a tetanus shot. We continued the shooting, and on one take I went to get Bullet from Dave to take out of the scene and I felt an incredible pressure on my left arm as if a vice had suddenly closed on it... then I felt the teeth.

When I reached out to take Bullet I had extended my arm out too much to Dave and Bullet, in "agitated mode," went for my arm. I continued to exit the scene as I was supposed to, but the trainers came in and stopped it and removed Bullet from my arm. We rolled up my sleeve and there was hardly anything there. There were two of the tiniest little bruises but my arm hurt like hell. It wasn't from the teeth but the pressure Bullet put on my forearm muscle. So, of course, I have to get a shot. I didn't want to but they insisted that I must. So, Dave and I became the favored actors, members of the same club, the "He who was attacked by the same dog" club. Quentin came over and said, "I only have my best guys attacked." On the way to the hospital, Dave and I wondered how they were going to react when we tell them he and I were attacked by the SAME DOG.

The hospital was a breeze. They were waiting for us and after filling out some simple papers, they gave us the shots and we were out of there. Dave went to his room but I absolutely HAD to get to a drugstore and get some gel foam foot inserts as the boots I have been wearing had become Viet Cong torture devices. It was unbearable. I felt like I was walking on wood turned sideways every step I took. I bought four pair, the idea being to put two in each boot.

Tuesday April 10th

We were picked up at 6 a.m., taken to the set, got in costume and this was a very fun day, all leading up to the dogs attacking D'Artagnan.

If you were to ask me what is it like to be directed by Quentin Tarantino, or ask what it is like on the set, I would have to say it is the most fun set I've ever been on. Everyone is in a good mood, especially Quentin. You hear him laugh all day. We would be sitting a hundred yards away in our little social area with our chairs away from the action, and we would hear Quentin laughing, from a small giggle to an uproarish gut-busting belly laugh.

Dave has been playing his character, Mr. Stonecipher, in a very dumb hillbilly, extremely slurred dialogue, lazy tongue sort of way, so much that Quentin and the crew and the actors are all picking up on it and imitating him. We call it "Stoneciphereeze." After one take, Quentin started talking in Stoneciphereeze, but we couldn't make out that he was saying "okay we got it." In a very slurred, dragged out, slow, lazy delivery he said, "bahhhht... wrrrrrrrrrrrr gahhhhnnnna dooo waannnnnnnnn mrrrrrrrrrrrrr."

After another take later in the day, Quentin, atop a tall ladder, announced, "Okay we got this... but we're going to do one more becaussssssseeeeee??????" And the whole cast and crew, including me, yelled out, "BECAUSEWELOVEMAKINGMOVIES!" What fun.

Tomorrow we are supposed to start the day with the dogs attacking and tearing D'Artagnan apart.

It's a strange sight to see all these director's chairs scattered around the swamp. Some have the actors' names on them and some just say "cast." We are just barely off a dirt road with enough solid ground to put the chairs up, and a medical cart, and beverage coolers, and loads of camera equipment, a crane, and costume racks, and lots and lots of horses, and the attack dogs' trailers.

Every now and then the snake handlers would come by with their probes and extended claw gizmos looking around our chairs for snakes. We are situated just a stone's throw away from the dense swamp on both sides of our little dirt road. It's a place I would not like to walk into. The snake handlers found three snakes, and they were not really big and not really deadly. They put one in a cloth bag and set it near the Trackers' shack. A bunch of us were sitting on our chairs and someone, a grip or P.A., came over and wanted to see the snake. The handler took it out of the bag and the grip actually taunted it. He started to do this "coochy coo" thing to the snake and it was amazing.

"The snake did an arched leap into the air and swung around and clamped and bit the grip on his hand."

The snake did an arched leap into the air and swung around and clamped and bit the grip on his hand. He screamed and jumped backwards. Another one headed to the tetanus shot clinic.

Wednesday April 11th.

This has been a fabulous day. We got rained out and had to quit early, but before that, we actually shot the dog attack on Ato, the guy playing D'Artagnan. The first set up was the dogs really attacking Ato though his arms and legs were padded and the dogs attacked the padding. As usual, his performance was awesome. He was screaming and crying, and it built to a point and then took on another dimension when he no longer yelled for mercy but did a high-pitched, painful scream for his life. Yesterday, his performance, crying and begging for mercy from Leonardo DiCaprio's character, Calvin Candie, was also awesome, and when he got in the van this morning with me and the trackers, we all told him so and he was elated.

Then it came time for the effects guys to attach the false arm to him for the dogs to rip off. He had to tuck his real arm behind him so the false arm looked like his real arm. When he laid down on the ground, you could pretty much see his real arm sticking out from under his back and it raised him slightly off the ground.

They did a few takes and the dogs really dragged him all over the place and his real arm kept coming out from under him. It happened on every take.

I was getting frustrated watching this because I was dying to make a suggestion but it's not my place. I am an actor on this picture and it's not my place to suggest effects stuff. Quentin looked a little frustrated but laughed a lot and told jokes as they set up again. He walked by me to tell me to mime the yelling when the dogs are attacking Ato as it might distract the dogs and turn them toward us trackers.

I reminded him that in *Day of the Dead,* I had to cut off a character's arm, a fake arm, and we dug a hole under him for his real arm behind his back to rest into, thus making him look level to the ground and making the fake arm look more like his real one. He said, "but the dogs drag Ato so much you might see the hole." I said with his real arm inside the hole it could help anchor him there. He liked that idea and I told him not to say it came from me. He laughed an understanding "I get it" kind of laugh and walked back toward the action.

Ten minutes later, he told them that they should dig a hole under Ato for his real arm behind his back, and once they did, it looked more real and his the fake arm looked very much like his real arm. The dogs attacked, and it worked and they were ready to move onto the next shot.

A few minutes later, Quentin walked up to me, and I felt him slip something into my hand. He said, "We have a tradition on my sets that when someone from another department helps out to solve a problem, they get five dollars. It's called the five dollar shot." I said that was really cool... and a cool thing to do. He said it's not always the case that an EXPERT on the problem of the other department steps up, and he just made my day. I'm going to frame that five dollars, but I have to get Quentin to sign it.

I have to say why this was such a thrilling experience for me. Quentin Tarantino, a long time ago before he did ANYTHING, came up to me at a horror convention in L.A. and said something like "Mr. Savini, I am such a big fan of yours, and I work in a video store in Manhattan Beach, and I was won-dering if you wouldn't mind coming there to see what we have... we have lots of your movies." And... I went. I saw him there and he showed me my movies and I signed a few. Then I would see him at a party at Greg Nicotero's house out there when I would visit, and he was just this big quiet guy who sat in a corner and was kind of just... there.

When he did *Reservoir Dogs,* I was pissed off and envious of him because this was the kind of movie I would make and that I wanted to make, with balls-out action and bad ass dialogue, and it just pissed me off that he did it first. But then, after *Pulp Fiction* and *Kill Bill* and *Inglorious Basterds,* I came to be a big fan of HIS, and I realized that he is a brilliant genius and his talent is overwhelming, and I grew to respect and admire him, so to have him listen to me on HIS set and honor me like that was so thrilling and made me feel terrific.

We were supposed to leave the next day, Thursday, but because we were rained out today, we were told we would have to come back tomorrow. It still means we can fly out Friday to get to Austin so I can play my part in the video game that will be called *Loco-Cycle.* I informed Bill Muehl, the game producer in Austin, that he should look for a back-up in case the schedule changes again because of weather.

Thursday April 12th
Our call was 5 a.m. this morning in order to get an early start on our last day here on the swamp set. At our trailer base camp and in costume, we were taken to breakfast and I have to say, for being out here in the middle of nowhere flanking a swamp, they are really taking care of us. Breakfast is whatever you want from a portable cooking trailer, and inside the building next door that is normally a tourist attraction called Swamp Tours, a pancake and waffle bar. Farther inside were rows of tables and chairs and a healthy breakfast buffet of fruits and yogurts and biscuits for "shit on a shingle" as we called it in the Army, and the biggest juicer I've ever seen and next to it, laid out in neat bins, were

carrots, apples, and an assortment of vegetables you can use to make your own healthy smoothie... and next to that was a huge orange juice squeezer and vat of fresh oranges. I made, as usual, the biggest glass of fresh squeezed orange juice, then went back in the van to the base camp trailers to grab my raccoon vest and off to the set.

Today was mostly standing on the set, off camera, to watch Leonardo DiCaprio and Christoph Waltz, and Jamie Foxx do their particular dialogue that leads up to us releasing the dogs onto Ato, or rather the runaway slave D'Artagnan. We, the Trackers, had no dialogue, except for Dave and his "Stonecipehereeze" exchange with Leonardo, who tells him to "Shut those goddamn dogs up... I can't hear myself think!"

Dave slurs the command to the dogs, one dog in particular named Marsha, and Leonardo comes out of his carriage and says to D'Artagnan that he paid five hundred dollars and he expects five fights. He asks if the slave is going to reimburse him and if he even knows what "reimburse" means. Jamie Foxx says no one is paying him anything and he's tired of this banter. Leonardo says he's never seen a "nigger" quite like Jamie and asks if he minds if he handles the situation in his own way. Jamie says that he doesn't mind, and Leonardo says to Dave in a low voice to "send D'Artagnan to nigger heaven."

The next shot is on James Parks holding his dog, as the trainers make the dog go berserk and he releases the dog toward the camera... then he does some kind of hillbilly dance of glee toward the camera and off. We all applauded. After more angles of slaves and overseers and other trackers reacting to the attack, and the camera high in the trees on a crane looking down on all of us reacting to the dog attack, it was time to point the camera toward me and Ted Neely as I held onto two dogs, Bullet and Hank, before releasing them toward

"It's amazing but in that outfit he looked as young as he did in Titanic."

the camera and to Tom Roach, the trainer. I worked out with Ted that after I released the dogs I would turn to him and in sign language hold my crotch and do the cut symbol indicating the dogs will tear off D'Artagnan's balls. The camera was on us now and the dogs attacked each other first. Then they pulled me to my knees, and on the third take I held them fast and did kind of a "hands carelessly in the air" release and did my bit with Ted. Quentin shot two takes of that, and then a take where he over-cranked the camera so the dogs would be running toward us in slow motion. And that was a wrap on us and the scene.

Leonardo came over dressed partly in his costume and in his own green and orange summery plaid shirt and said he wanted to get a shot "with his Trackers." It's amazing but in that outfit he looked as young as he did in Titanic: fresh faced and his hair hanging down over his face. We all lined up with him for the still camera guy and then one of the dog trainers came over to hand him a dog. He looked right at me and we exchanged a wide eyed look of "Uh Oh!" but all went well and when the shot was over he looked at me again and said, "I'm not moving," and he was frozen still until the trainer came over and took the dog.

The next morning, we flew to Austin, Texas where I was to play a character in a video game called *LocoCycle*... but that's another story.

July 24th

Yep, it's been around 3 months since I left the set in New Orleans, and I am now in Los Angeles to continue shooting *Django Unchained*. In the interim I went to Austin, Texas to shoot *Machete Kills*, but that's another journal. I was a little shocked to learn from the other cast members that it's been three months. In fact, I've been seeing the trailer for *Django*... IN THE THEATERS... and would casually turn to whoever I was with and say, "We're still shooting this."

I told Quentin tonight that people are already quoting the movie, like Leonardo DeCaprio's line, "Gentlemen, you had my curiosity, now you have my attention." He said it hasn't been since *Butch Cassidy and the Sundance Kid* that audiences are so anxiously awaiting the release of a Western.

Well, I have been here since Tuesday, the 17th, and every day I got a text telling me we were not going to shoot the next day. They brought me out to Los Angeles just in case they needed to shoot our scene. When I say "our," I mean the Trackers'. So, I've been on a little vacation here for a week with Jodii, my girlfriend from Australia who has also returned to me in the interim. My best friend Rob Lucas has also arrived in L.A. and is renting a house and moved here from Connecticut. His furniture arrives tomorrow. He has given me a bed room in his house so I can come to L.A. more often, especially in audition season.

So, we have spent the last week with him, as he has booked a room near us in Valencia until the moving truck arrives at his new house. He has been driving us all over the place: the Goodwill store in Beverly Hills, shopping on Melrose Avenue, dinner at the Rainbow on Sunset, dinner at the Smokehouse in Burbank, dinner at Musso and Frank's, shopping on Hollywood Boulevard, and a visit with Bob Burns and his fabulous collection of Hollywood memorabilia... and ending last night with Rob inviting seventeen of our close friends out here to IRIS, the new Cirque De Soleil show at the Kodak Theater, home to the Academy Awards ceremony. This has been one fantastic visit to L.A., in preparation to finishing up *Django*.

Tonight, we started with we trackers playing cards inside the real Trackers' House we use in New Orleans. They tore down and packed up the real Trackers House we used in the swamp in New Orleans and rebuilt it here inside one of the sound stages at the Santa Clarita Studios. It was me and James Parks and Mike Bowen playing cards, with Big Jake on our left building a bird house, Dave Steen taking a bath in a big wooden tub, and Ted Neeley sitting in a rocking chair playing a mouth harp. We are using slave ears as money in the card game.

Earlier tonight, Quentin had a meeting with the card players and taught us a card game involving diamonds, hearts, clubs, spades, and facecards. He told us to go practice the game before shooting and

"We are using slave ears as money in the card game."

that turned into each of us inventing schtick to do while we were playing, but when it came time to shoot it, we started playing it legitimately, but soon were just throwing any card we could grab into the game as Quentin wanted us to play it quicker. It's just a set up to keep all of us doing something before Jamie Foxx, Django, comes in and blows us all away.

After a few takes of the card game, with the camera on a circular track to move around the table, we were free for a few hours before we were called back in to be squibbed. That means the explosives inside blood packs were taped inside our clothing and rigged to explode in a very bloody way when Django shoots us. I had two on my chest and when they blow I'm supposed to fly backwards with my chair away from the card table. Jake had two on his chest and his were to go off first, then me, then James, who had one on his chest and one on his back. Mike had one in his hat, and the last was Zoe Bell who had two on her chest.

This was all rigged to happen .... ALL AT ONCE, in the same camera set up, one right after another, and in between us getting shot, cards and bottles and potatoes on the table and walls were rigged to explode. I was hearing nightmares from Greg Funk and Big Jake about others who were squibbed having to do it over and over again. One guy seven times. I knew there would be a lot of sticky blood all over the place and the idea of doing it over and over again was not something I relished.

While they were setting this up, Quentin announced that the previous shot we did, the card game, was the 1600th set up for the movie... WITH ONE CAMERA. He was very proud of that and should be, as he was in charge of every framing. He framed every single shot in the film. The B camera only was on set up 95. I was surprised that after he said that he looked at me and said I should do that on *Children Shouldn't Play With Dead Things*. He was referring to the remake I am scheduled to direct before the end of the year. He said it's one of his favorite films and even offered me Bob Clark's script that he wrote just before he died.

It was getting close to shoot what would be a magnificent scene of all of us getting shot to death. I was practicing pushing myself backward when my squibs go off, and James was practicing what he would do, and Mike was anticipating how he would fall, and I could feel my heart beating faster and faster, as soon Quentin would call action and all hell will break lose. It's one thing to shoot squibs going off on one person, but multiple squibs going off on five people? Plus the cards on the table and the bottles and the potatoes in a dish and the walls around us at the same time. My heart was beating faster and faster... what if I can't fly backwards at the right timing, what if Jake crashes into the table behind him and sends it crashing into my face as I lay there, or James falls on me when I am pretending to be dead, or Zoe steps on me as she attempts to attack Django with a knife before he shoots her??? All these thoughts were rushing through my head and before I knew it, Quentin called action, and everything in life went into slow motion.

Jamie Foxx's stand-in was at the camera firing very loud full loads at us with his revolver... I saw Big Jake get hit and fly backwards onto the table with the bird house, the potatoes exploded on the table, and I felt my chest explode and my legs immediately propelled me backward and I don't even remember hitting the floor, and as I laid there I could feel and see many explosions and debris and blood flying all over us. Quentin called "Cut" and we all laid still so the photographers could take our pictures, and then Quentin said it was so fabulous we don't need to do it again. We all wanted to hug him, and some of us did because we wouldn't have to go through that again. We all went home high as kites to have just been part of movie history. Violent, Western, *Wild Bunch*, Quentin Tarantino, 1601 setups with one camera, movie history.

It's December now, and my friend producer Mike Ruggiero invited me to come up to New York for a Producer's Guild screening of *Django*

with Quentin in attendance. I of course drove the six hours to New York for such an experience.

We got terrific seats in the front row of the bleacher style seating by sneaking into the theater early and grabbing the ones that were not saved for Miramax.

The movie blew everyone away, Mike and I included, and when it came time for the Q and A with Quentin, I was the first to raise my hand. The moderator was a film critic for the *Village Voice* and he said, "That looks like Tom Savini, "and Quentin said, "Yes it IS" and told the audience I was one of the Trackers in the film and there was a bit of applause but I motioned it away and told Quentin that "He blowed up real good." I then asked if he was also the guy in the bag/hood who says, "We don't have any extra bags." He said it was him and then did all the lines he said as that character. I told him that *Django* is a beautiful love story.

He was asked by somebody what he was going to do next, and he said he will probably do a lot of writing and maybe experiment with a different genre... probably an all out horror movie. I screamed "YES!!!!!" and he said, "Ha! Savini likes that idea."

We saw him outside getting into an SUV and I yelled "QT?" He turned and we hugged, and he asked if we liked the movie, and I said I will probably see it ten times. I've seen it five times so far.

Lost Boys: The Tribe Journals

Journal One

I got the call from Greg Nicotero: "Hey, they want you to be in *Lost Boys II*." Lovely, I get to be a vampire again sometime in September, but first I have to go be a vampire in *The Dead Matter*, a movie directed by Ed of *Midnight Syndicate*, "The greatest original horror movie music in the Universe." I used to go by their table at conventions when they had customers and yell that as I walked by. This endeared me to them, and they hired me to play Sebed in their first horror movie. Cut to now as I sit in a great hotel suite in Vancouver, British Columbia, Canada, on a Sunday morning. Vancouver is the new Hollywood and I found out yesterday there are 37 movie studios here: just here! I was watching a biography of Bruce Lee in this room yesterday narrated by Miguel Ferrer and then I went down to the gym. I'm working out and in walked Miguel Ferrer. Yep, the new Hollywood. He's up here shooting the new *Bionic Woman* television series.

"I hate fake blood."

The flight up here was uneventful, short and smooth and first class pleasant.

Immigration, however was a nightmare. It was hours of sitting there among hundreds of Asian students coming in. I also learned that Vancouver is 40% Asian. I was able to eliminate the distress by pretending I was watching a comedy, as the customs officers kept calling names like Wang and Lee and Liu and nobody responded. They had to keep yelling their names and try different pronunciations before anybody would respond. I kept thinking, Jesus Christ, you're coming into a new country and you're here to get OUT of here: pay attention! That is, until I decided this is a comedy, and I got up to complain that new entry papers were put on top of the ones already there, where mine were, by newly entering customs officers. They picked out my papers, and I paid the work permit fee and went to look for my luggage. There were dozens of baggage carousels filled with overflowing bags. I walked among the towering moving bags thinking of the hours that were going to go by as I searched for my bags and I swear to God, I looked down and there coming right at me was my bag. I guess I still have my luck.

The hotel is right in the middle of town and it's like being in the middle of Manhattan or Toronto with lots of shops and restaurants and one of the first things I did was buy an expensive watch. It is my "I don't give a fuck that I was just robbed" watch, and every time I look at it, it gives me strength and restores my confidence and makes me feel less violated. Before I came up here, my house was broken into and they stole my safe. I say "they" because my safe weighed over 350 pounds, and they just walked in and took it with my life savings in cash, which was my grandson's college education and what I would have left Lia if anything were to happen to me. I kept it in my safe so that Lia would have instant access to it: No Executor of will or red tape or IRS: instant access. Well, not anymore. It's all gone. I'm not going to get another safe if they can just walk in and take it like that. I would have been better off putting it behind some books or up the ass of my full size Darth Vader stature or anywhere else but the SAFE. You know, where it's supposed to be SAFE! I would still have it if it hadn't been in the first place they would look for it.... in the fucking SAFE!

I try to look for any good that could come out of a problem or a challenge, and for days, I just couldn't think of any. I could see how easy it would be to fall into a depression over it if I let my thoughts take me there. A long time ago, I learned to control my thoughts and not let them control me. Control your thoughts and you control your life. Change your thoughts and you change your life. When the thoughts of this disaster would come at me, and they came at me a lot, I decided not to give them my time. I actually said "shut up" to them and they went away. Anyway, the good that came out of this disaster is the realization that the real treasures in life are not what you put in a safe and can be taken away; the real treasures of life are your friends and family and nothing can take that away. It was Greg Nicotero and Jeff Imbrescia who helped me find the good in all this. Jeff, the president and owner of my makeup effects program, gave me an advance on my consultation fee, and Greg, out of the blue, sent me a check to help with living expenses and carry on and led me to this job here in Vancouver playing a vampire in the new *Lost Boys II* movie. The first check from the movie allowed me to buy the watch.

Journal Two

I hate fake blood.

It's icky and gooey and the worst thing about it is that it's so fucking sticky. I hate being sticky. My nightmares are being sticky like under the armpits, or between my fingers, or behind the knees, you know, anywhere you bend and flesh touches flesh, and sticky. I hate it... I just can't stand it and really hate it. Even the smallest amount on me makes my skin crawl and sends the most uncomfortable goose bumpy hair standing on end and a queasy jittery feeling up and down my spine. By the end of this night, I will be swimming in fake blood. Aghhhhhhhhhhhh.

Early on tonight, I got to meet and rehearse my fight with the Lost Boys: Kyle, Sean, Merwin, and Angus. Those are their real names and not the characters they play. Merwin is a very light skinned

192

Jamaican... or wait... he corrected me.... "Saint Lucian": whatever that is. He has a shaved head and a goatee that zigzags across his lower jaw and is very well built. He's in terrific shape, as they all are gorgeous physical specimens. Kyle is the boy next door with a great sense of humor, and Angus is a Sutherland, a half-brother of Kiefer, tall with shoulder-length curly blonde hair. He is soft-spoken and mostly quiet. Sean is about my height, and his face and every gesture, every smile, every word reminds you of Brad Pitt. He says he gets that a lot. He is very bright and thoughtful and thorough, and he points to the night sky to show us how close Venus is tonight.

I rehearsed the fight alone with Garvin the stunt co-ordinator. He is my height, well-built, and said he hopes to be in my shape when he is sixty. The fight is a lot of pushing and using the weight of my opponents against them as I throw them into each other before they overpower and attack me. We created the sequence and later show it to the Lost Boys when they arrive. Angus is the ring-leader and just stands as his boys attack. Everyone contributed something to what Garvin and I put together, and P.J. Pesce, the

"Sean says, 'Fuck that, Suck my dick.'"

director, was called in to see it. He liked it fine and wanted to make sure it is like a hyena attack on a lion. He saw one in South Africa and that's what he wants this opening sequence in the film to be.

We split up afterward.... they to their trailers and me into the mansion on the sea that is to be mine in the film. This place is incredible. Huge, like a modern resort. The master bathroom has a 42-inch plasma television embedded into the wall opposite the toilet. The shower is a Plexiglas enclosure about eight feet square and the water shoots at you from everywhere: head, foot, above, below. Never saw anything like it. The water in the swimming pool is on the level with the ground around it. No ledge, no steps....just the ground, the concrete and the water. One edge of the pool is where the water overflows into a grid and then is re-circulated into the pool. It was an infinity pool is constantly overflowing.

My first scene tonight is me looking over the balcony at the Lost Boys who have invaded my property and have been surfing on my beach. The mansion is nowhere near the ocean, but the crew erected a huge green screen flat and put sand in front of it for the LOST BOYS in their wetsuits to play in front of with their surf boards. Later, they will CGI the ocean and moon and the surf and the reflections. P.J. does a long shot and then a close up of me on the balcony, and I wear sunglasses that also have a green solid color so later he can put in a reflection in the glasses of what I see. P.J is a card... literally. He carries a deck of cards with him and is constantly doing one handed cutting and shuffling. We are both card-carrying members of the Magic Castle in Hollywood. It's a private club/mansion on a hill behind the Chinese Theater solely for magicians. He is constantly showing me some trick and I would arrive on the set with a trick or two to show him. We connected and hit it off splendidly. Soon, I am down on the makeshift beach with the Lost Boys and rehash the fight scene on the sand. Then, on "action," my line is, "What the fuck are you doing on my beach" Merwin says something like "Fuck your mother" or grabbing his balls, "I got your beach right here" or some mumbo jumbo I don't understand, and Sean says, laughing, "He says

it's not your beach." I say, "Is that a fact? Let me tell you something: I own every drop of water from here to the lighthouse, as well as the sand and everything that's on it, which I guess NOW means you."

Sean says, "Fuck that," and "Suck my dick" and heads past me with his surfboard. I do a one handed shove into his chest, knocking him off his feet, and he lands on his back in the tall soft grass. Kyle approaches me and says, "No need to get rough: we're all done anyway." I say, "Uh uh: we're just getting started" and I turn into a vampire. First they shot me normal saying that and then with my fangs and black contact lenses. They will morph me into a vampire later.

All hell breaks loose as Kyle attacks me and I use his weight against him with an Aikido move and throw him into Merwin and Angus. Sean jumps on my back and I throw him off, and in an instant,

Merwin and Kyle and Sean attack me knocking me off my feet onto a mat covered with cold wet grass. We do that a few times and now it's time for the blood. I have been dreading this all night as I knew it was inevitable that I am going to be sticky. I am nice and warm under the big coat that wardrobe gave me to stave off the cold, and I am quite comfortable. I am counting the seconds before I know I am going to feel the first wave of a bloody attack from the boys.

Kyle fills his mouth with fake blood and on "action," I am supposed to resist their attack and Kyle is to force my head down and put his mouth on my neck and bite and spurt the blood as if it is coming out of me. On "action," I feel his beard stubble scratching my neck and his mouth on me, and suddenly, the air explodes around my face and neck with the first bloodletting. We all go into the heated tent to stay warm, only now I am freezing with sticky fake blood

all over my neck and running down my back. On the next take, Sean is fitted with tubes up each sleeve so the effects guys can pump blood out of his hands while he attacks me, plus Kyle once again does the mouth blood spurt on my neck. On "action," this time I feel the blood on my neck, and suddenly I am given a blood enema and then I feel it
surging up my back and down my legs.

I am completely drenched with gallons of blood coursing all through my clothing. Greg Nicotero would love to see all this blood all over me. Once again we are led to the heated tent. As I stand there I feel like a huge pancake with sticky syrup flowing down my body, heated by the glowing propane heater in the heated tent. The effects guys enter the tent and they are now to fit me into this overshirt that has a fake chest attached to it. I am so covered with blood that as they fit this shirt over me, it feels like I am naked and trying to stuff myself into a huge cinnamon bun, icing on the inside. I am in hell. Somebody please kill me.

This time on "action," the Lost Boys tear into my chest, pulling my ribs apart and ripping out my guts. I can feel myself floating now on the new blood that has been pumped into and around and under the chest. It has flowed toward my neck and around it and behind me and under my back, and down the front of my underwear and down my legs and behind me. I am really floating now in a pool of blood. When it's over they want me to go to the tent and I say, "I'm not moving." I'd rather lie here in this blood than feel what it's like to get up and move. I am now violently shaking on the verge of hypothermia and they bring out heaters and surround me with them and cover me with blankets. I stop shaking and I ask if they could be ready after this next take with the knife gag to cut off my head, as I just want to lie there.

A strange feeling overtakes me. I am lying there in a pool of blood looking up at the stars in the night sky, and I feel like an accident victim. Peo-

"The Lost Boys tear into my chest, pulling my ribs apart and ripping out my guts..."

ple come into my view to cover me with blankets or to keep me warm and I am all bloody. I feel like some horrible thing has happened to me and we are just waiting for the ambulance.

On "action," Kyle comes in and as I try to weakly fight him off, he starts cutting my throat with a specially prepared knife as blood shoots out of the blade. We do a few takes of this and I am finished and can go to the showers at the side of the pool. I weigh about fifty pounds more now with the blood filled fake chest and getting that off was the stickiest feeling of my life. Nothing has ever felt so good as that hot water from that shower washing that sticky icky red goo off of me and down the drain.

While I shower they continue the scene with my fake head as Sean says, "Hey guys, watch this," and punts my head into the imaginary ocean. It's on a fishing line from a fishing rod and someone reels it back in for more takes.

I got home to the hotel and turned up the heat and snuggled into my warm bed, appreciating it more that ever remembering the pool of blood I was floating in an hour ago.

Scrapbook

Wearing George Romeo's glasses at some convention

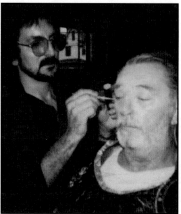

Preparing Robert Mitchum to receive a bloody nose for *Maria's Lovers*

With Eiza Gonzales in *Dusk til Dawn the TV series*

Birthday present from Greg Nicotero

197

My favorite picture with Taso

Refurbishing the Leatherface mask with assistant
Jason Baker

Rare one of a kind prototypes from beloved Henry Alvarez

The Pinhead Experience

Some of the half masks I created for Trick Or Treat Studios

198

Greg Nicotero presents me with a Lifetime Achievment Award
at the Sitges Film Festival in Spain

With Rick Baker at Monsterpalooza

The one and only Dick Smith doing portfolio review at my school

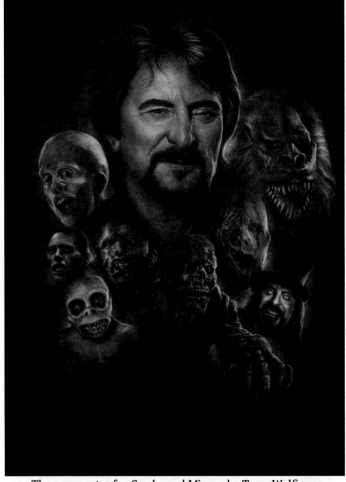

The new poster for *Smoke and Mirrors* by Terry Wolfinger

At my special makeup effects school with my pet gorilla

As The Amazing Savini for Epix Drive-In

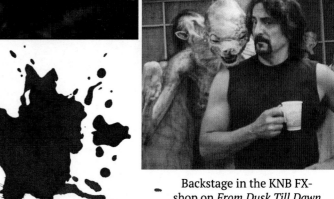

Visiting Salma Hayek on
the set of *Dogma*

Backstage in the KNB FX-
shop on *From Dusk Till Dawn*

The traditional yearly birthday photos

Some of my action figures are life size

Sculpting Buttons

With Boris, the dummy I created
for *Dawn of The Dead*

Sculpting Lizzy

Dad Visits *Creepshow* set

Rare *Dawn of The Dead photo*. Marty Schiff, Tony Buba and Nick Tallo

My grandson, James, and Lia

My son, Lon, and family

My daughters Audrey, Katarina, and Lia

Lia with George

Arnold

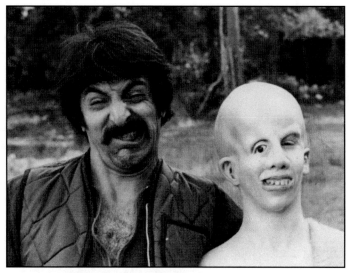

Ari Lehman during the original *Friday the 13th*

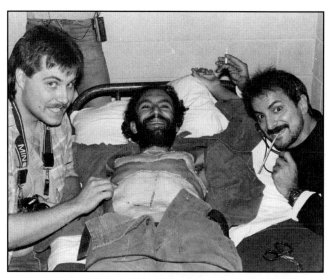

John Vulich and Tim DeLeo From *Day of the Dead*

Never before seen photo
of us preparing Joe Pilato

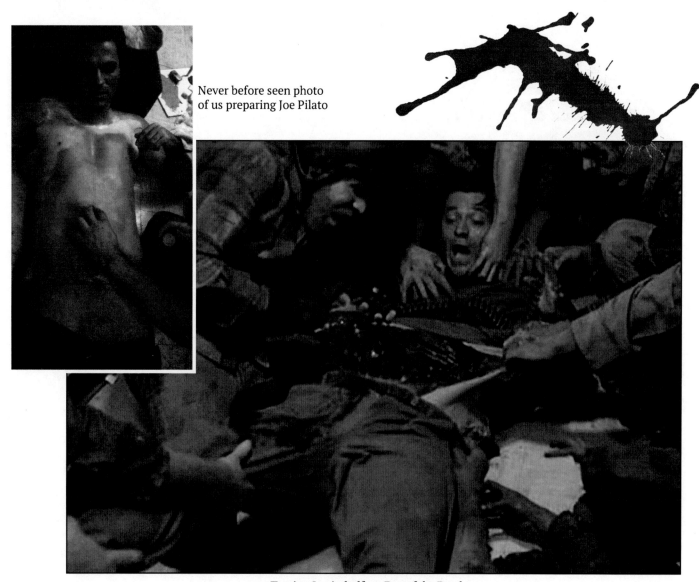

Tearing Joe in half on *Day of the Dead*

203

Mark Tierno

Okay, I'll finally admit I was on the set of *Nightmare*

Goofing on Greg *Day of Dead*

Patty and Bill on *Night of the Living Dead (1990)*

Bruce Campbell

George giving me a headlock

Ari Lehman

Comedy-Tragedy

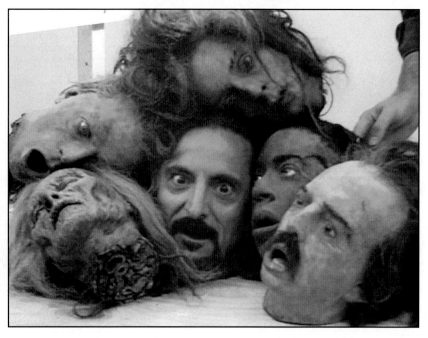

Halloween 1985

Dick Smith, the greatest makeup artist ever

Greg Nicotero came over to play

Me in the *Dusk Till Dawn TV Series*

Venice Beach with Rob Lucas, Tyler and Nikki, Mike Ruggiero

206

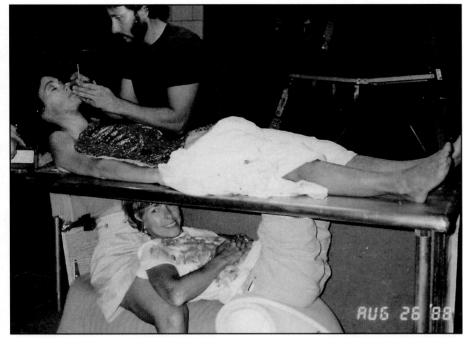

Magic

The last huge set piece from the chariot
race in Ben Hur-Cinecetta studios in Rome

Filmography

DIRECTOR *(DGA)* **ACTOR** *(SAG, AFTRA)*

MOVIES:
- NIGHT OF THE LIVING DEAD '90
- THEATRE BIZARRE

- DJANGO UNCHAINED
- THEATRE BIZARRE
- LAND OF THE DEAD
- DEMENTONS
- INNOCENT BLOOD
- LOST BOYS: THE TRIBE
- FROM DUSK TILL DAWN
- FROM DUSK TILL DAWN: TV SERIES
- MACHETE/MACHETE KILLS
- INHUMAN RESOURCES
- CREEPSHOW/CREEPSHOW II
- DAWN OF THE DEAD (ORIGINAL)
- DAWN OF THE DEAD (REMAKE)
- PERKS OF BEING A WALLFLOWER
- ZACK AND MIRI MAKE A PORNO

- GRINDHOUSE
- MANIAC
- MARTIN
- MR. STITCH
- KNIGHTRIDERS
- THE SIMPSONS

TV:
- TALES FROM THE DARKSIDE
- TOM SAVINI'S CHILL FACTOR
- CREEPSHOW TV

STAGE:
- TOM SAVINI'S DRACULA

SPECIAL MAKEUP EFFECTS:

- FRIDAY THE 13TH
- FRIDAY THE 13TH IV
- DAWN OF THE DEAD
- DAY OF THE DEAD
- MANIAC
- EYES OF A STRANGER
- THE BURNING
- THE PROWLER
- SLIPKNOT: Corey Taylor Masks

- DERANGED
- DEATH DREAM
- MARTIN
- MARIA'S LOVERS
- CREEPSHOW
- TWO EVIL EYES
- TRAUMA
- INVASION USA
- WWE (Triple H Crown)

- TRAUMA
- NECRONOMICON
- RED SCORPION
- MONKEY SHINES
- TEXAS CHAINSAW MASSACRE II
- MR. STITCH
- KILLING ZOE
- EFFECTS

- FRIDAY THE 13TH VIDEO GAME: The kills and Savini Jason

GRANDE ILLUSIONS

The Art and Technique of Special Make-Up Effects
Original Books I & II

From The Films of
TOM SAVINI

Forewords by: Stephen King, George Romero and Dick Smith

Made in the USA
Monee, IL
08 September 2022

d982bcbb-964a-4abf-a141-0e846d1a3f38R01